WRITE YOUR WAY THROUGH CHANGE

A 21-DAY DEVOTIONAL JOURNAL FOR GRIEF AND MAJOR LIFE TRANSITIONS

JANET HANEY

CONTENTS

JOIN ME FOR A FREE JOURNALING CLASS!

Thanks for picking up *Write Your Way Through Change*. This book came about from teaching online creative journaling classes. These classes are laid-back, safe places to share and explore your journaling practice.

I occasionally teach a _free_ class for those interested in knowing more.

To sign up for the next free class, go to...

http://www.jhaney.com/join

You'll be on the list to get more info.

LET'S WRITE!

I share my story and dedicate this book to you,

so you can share your own story.

ACKNOWLEDGMENTS

There are people who show up in your life, who mark you and change your world. I have met such a one. We have never been in the same room together or even the same state, but our weekly meeting over the internet airwaves has established a firm foundation.

She is wise, talented, and creative. She has given me the structure to make hard decisions and given legs to this book. But mostly she has taught me to be brave. Through her example and gentle spirit, I have moved higher on the courage scale.

Thank you, Emily Ann Peterson, for being you and taking me on. I've been made a better person.

MEET THE AUTHOR

I'm Janet Haney, an author and creative journaling teacher based out of northern Kentucky, USA. I'm also living proof that writing can help anyone through grief and transitions.

Believe me, life doesn't turn out the way we think it will. We often have a vision of how we think it will look. But when unexpected tragedies and grief happen, we feel somehow cheated or discouraged.

Our pain, struggles, or grief clog our hearts. Nothing in life is wasted, not even our struggles. They can point to our true calling in life.

Times of transition and these "hard places" can actually become a treasure. It doesn't feel like that in the moment, but suffering *can* have a purpose if we seek out that purpose.

NEW BEGINNINGS CAN HAPPEN ANYWHERE ALONG THE WAY.

INTRODUCTION

Change occurs in all cultures, across every historical period, in every species, and in every human being. It begins the moment we're conceived and ends when we take our last breath.

Welcome and essential change can be marvelous, but unwanted change can bring devastation and grief. Any kind of life transition requires adjustment. It takes picking up a new way of thinking that can seem slippery and hard to hold.

When we experience change, it's important to take stock of its effect on our lives. A peek into the whirlwind of change can open the way to consider new options. Investigating your feelings and thoughts is an important process to tackle, even in the most painful circumstances.

As I traveled the various trials in my life, I discovered how much it helped to have an outlet for the storms that raged inside.

I've buried a son who died in his sleep at age 9. My husband began his battle with prostate cancer two years later. He fought long and hard, and eventually succumbed. I began a battle with breast cancer a few years later. My daughter moved out of state for career reasons to discover her own life. After my mastectomy, I found myself alone in a very empty nest.

THE EMPTY PAGE CAN HEAL

Understandably, I needed a place to spill the pain so I wouldn't drown in it. The empty page was that place. That's how I came to write my first book, *Hello Nobody: Standing at the Door Alone - What to Do When Everything Changes*.

At the end of each chapter in *Hello Nobody*, I posed several questions for further exploration and contemplation. I heard from so many readers that those questions helped them on their own journeys while reading about mine.

For some people, staring at a blank page only produces more anxiety. I've felt that way, too. I've wished there was someone who would say, "Ask me about that!" so I could tell my story. This is why I created the *Write Your Way Through Change* devotional journal.

In the midst of my darkest moments, I knew there must be others who, when faced with a difficult time in life, needed someone to sit beside them and help pull the threads attached to the pain or confusion. A whole sweater can be unraveled by gently pulling on the yarn at a broken stitch.

While I was writing this devotional journal, I did my best to imagine you and the circumstances that bring you here to these empty pages.

I ask questions through the following pages, and I share my own answers as if I were sitting across the table listening to you share your journey. It's important to have someone to talk to during these seasons, and I'm happy to be that person for you throughout this book.

HOW TO USE THIS DEVOTIONAL JOURNAL

This journal is for *you*. Please use it however you'd like.

In the following pages, you'll find twenty-one segments, divided into 3 weeks. Each "day" contains four writing prompts and an additional four corresponding topical quotes. If you choose to use the entire book, you get over 160 writing prompts.

You could spend 21 days randomly picking a favorite prompt or quote. You could take 160 days to complete all of them. You could go through this book four times, once a quarter for a year, or anything in between! Tackle the material one day at a time or go at your own pace.

HOW TO USE A WRITING PROMPT

This kind of writing is meant for telling *your* story. These journal prompts are meant to unlock whatever writing needs to fall to the page. Write until your pen tells you to stop for the day. Some days will result in more words than others. This is normal. Some people like to use the prompts as a springboard to continue writing about different subjects. Again, this is up to you.

There's a great benefit to having a specific page to decant your reactions, insights, and feelings. It's like pouring a bottle of red wine into a larger container. A fine vintage requires room to breathe and bloom. The wine is given space for flavors to open up and become more vibrant. Decanting also separates any sediment that has collected as a wine sits and ages.

These prompts and pages can be a place to settle out sediment, open new flavors, and brighten spots in your life. They can give you the space to unpack your thoughts, especially the ones folded and tucked away in the drawer of grief or change. There's healing in telling your story, regardless of how the words come out.

Let them flow and become whatever you need them to be: challenging and insightful or introspective and searching.

My hope is that they allow a crack of light to shine into your heart for answers or understanding. I also hope that you are inspired and encouraged by looking at the life transitions or grief that you are facing.

WE ALL HAVE A STORY TO TELL

I believe we all have stories to share with the world, because someone out there needs to hear them. If you choose to share yours, you'll first need to know that story for yourself.

This journal just might be the beginning of getting it onto paper.

*L*et's write.

WEEK ONE

"When we are no longer able to change a situation, we are challenged to change ourselves.

~ Vicktor E. Frankl

CHANGE SHIFTS

> *Change isn't always for the worst; the shell that forms around a piece of sand looks to some people like an irritation, and to others, like a pearl.*
>
> ~ Jodi Picoult, *My Sister's Keeper*

It wasn't that long ago when I realized there is a specific process involved in moving through a major life transition. Any change in life, be it positive or negative, begins with a profound beginning and ends with a lasting outcome.

Changes in life can creep in as a welcome relief or a devastating blow that no one saw coming. Many of the major life changes I rode into as if on a paper glider someone had tossed into the air. The dips and turns were dictated by the curve of the wing or the wind that came up. I was not the pilot and felt no control in the landing. Sometimes my landing was on soft grass; other times, I took a nose-dive straight to the ground, ending in a crashed heap.

As I've lived through some major life-altering changes, I've become braver and stronger. Realizing the ride through these days, especially the hardest times, reveals the most important parts of who we are. God will use hard times to teach us lessons we couldn't know any other way. That makes them brilliant and gives purpose to the times that make no sense.

Change comes packaged in all shapes and sizes, and life has a way of unfolding certain boxes for each of us. Throughout this week, take notice of how grief is shifting and changing in your life.

DAY 1: SMALL VESSELS OF CHANGE

When thinking of the change in my life, I've felt the highest highs and the deepest depths. I had certain expectations of how life would be, and it has turned out to be nothing like I imagined. Perhaps the same is true for you.

Some of the changes I've experienced have changed me. Lessons born from struggle are the hardest to navigate, yet they grow the deepest roots.

Scripture reminds us that these times are not wasted by saying,

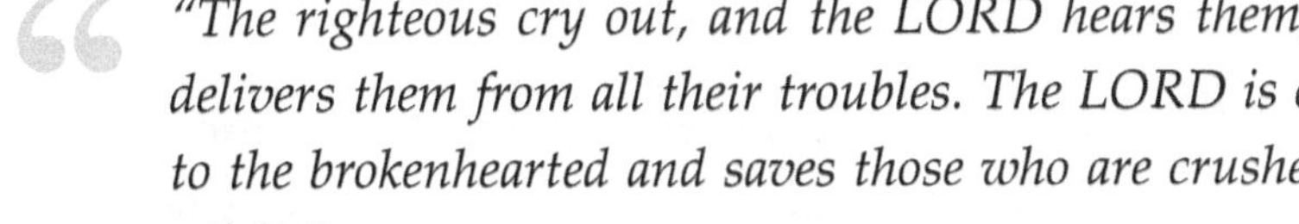

"The righteous cry out, and the LORD hears them; He delivers them from all their troubles. The LORD is close to the brokenhearted and saves those who are crushed in spirit."

Psalm 34:17-18 (New King James Version)

I had to come to terms with the way my difficult times unfolded. I wanted my husband healed from cancer and my son to have a long, healthy life. That was not the way things worked out.

My roots of faith were small and shallow at the start, but grew deep and strong, born out of pain and sorrow. The times of crushing and brokenness become the very thing God uses to sit a little closer and hold us a little tighter. We are promised deliverance from our troubles, but that doesn't necessarily mean our troubles are lifted. It means we are given what we need to travel through hard days and come to know God in a deeper way. Look for Him in your trials. He's there and will see your tears and hear your cries.

LIFE IS A TWO-SIDED COIN.

Pure joy can come from a deep place of change, such as the one that comes on your daughter's wedding day. There is both a 'hello' and a 'goodbye' spoken in the same breath. I might say hello to a new son in my life and goodbye to a daughter who previously belonged only to me.

Changes we've experienced carry an added burden or luxury of memory. When we look back, the memories and emotions they carry can be as real as the season in our lives when we experienced them.

God designed us to carry in our minds and hearts the past as we've lived it. He wants to show us He is the master designer of all and that our lives are richly textured with countless opportunities for Him to shine through. Even when we aren't looking for it, the past is a valuable canvas that paints God's faithfulness.

Just before the sun sets, the sky is painted in jewel colors. It's as if God splashes the horizon with brilliance to remind us of His love. Then he sends stars in the heavens for a reminder that, especially in the darkest times, He has guard over us.

TODAY, IS THE START OF THIS JOURNAL.

It's a place to spread out the life changes or grief that fill you and give it some perspective. It's like standing on the beach staring out across the ocean. You can look past the constant pounding waves that crash onto the shore to see an expanse of smooth or rough blue water that seems to have no end. It stretches to the horizon and is filled with all kinds of unknown adventures or perils.

We can climb into our small boat these next few days and paddle out to the safe, deep waters of our experiences. The next pages hold the promise of warm understanding, with maybe a catch of clarity.

PROMPTS 1-4

PROMPT 1

Let's write

Imagine you have rowed your small boat over the crashing surf, with skill and determination, and now find yourself in the smooth, calm sea just beyond the shore. You have all day to spend exploring the ocean around you.

Where do you go? What do you do? Who joins you?

Describe all that unfolds.

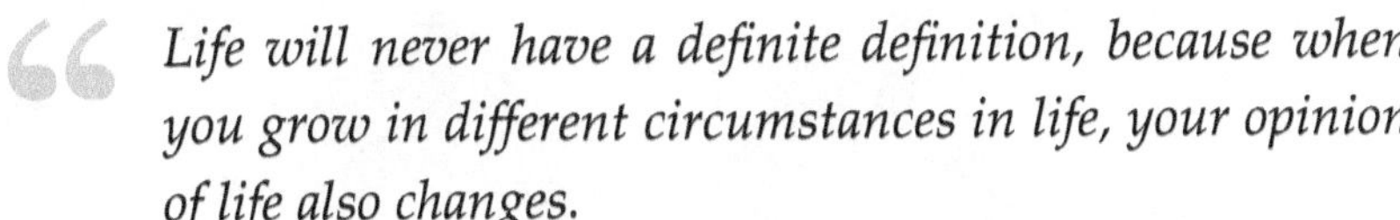

Life will never have a definite definition, because when you grow in different circumstances in life, your opinion of life also changes.

~ Unknown

PROMPT 2

Let's write.

Are there times in your life when you rocked the boat?

What was the outcome?

 *Only the guy who isn't rowing has time to rock the boat.*

~ Jean-Paul Sartre

PROMPT 3

Let's write.

Think about the journey you find yourself in.

Are you looking at the end result?

Are you looking at the travel it takes to get there?

 *It is good to have an end to journey toward; but it is the journey that matters, in the end.*

~ Ernest Hemingway

PROMPT 4

Let's write.

Everyone's faced difficult circumstances. You probably have some "battle scars" to prove it.

How have those circumstances changed you? Explain.

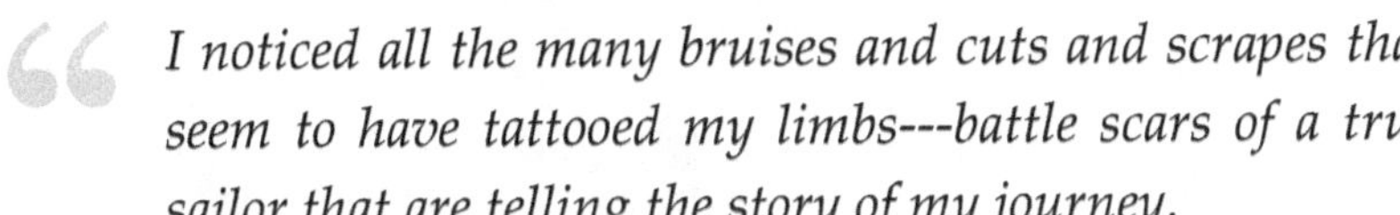

> *I noticed all the many bruises and cuts and scrapes that seem to have tattooed my limbs---battle scars of a true sailor that are telling the story of my journey.*

~ Michelle Segrest

DAY 2: POSITIVE AND NEGATIVE CHANGE

Moving to a new city for a job, seen as a positive change, can leave you feeling isolated and desperately alone in a new city. A new baby is a bundle of joy and a blessing, yet at the same time, can turn a family's world upside down, requiring adjustments at every turn.

This dichotomy is not uncommon. A diagnosis of breast cancer crashed my world for a season, but I realized first-hand how precious and precarious life is. I've tried to live more intentionally because of that journey. We can be brave in a crisis and fearful of a good thing; both reactions are legitimate responses.

So, on this hike together, I want you to relax and be assured that there are no wrong ways to feel or to process the circumstances you are marching through now. Both sides of a dollar bill are valuable.

THE POSITIVE AND NEGATIVE

When I think of a change in my life, certain words come to mind: *altered* or *broken, restored* or *replaced.* A new beginning brings *upheaval* or *a shift* in the way my life is unfolding. The end of a relationship, a role, or a purpose can lead to a difficult period of adjustment.

God can use this time to polish the tarnished spots that dull and darken the brilliance grief and heartache take from us. Tarnish appears as a layer of discoloration. It's a natural process, but it must be removed if the original shine is to return. God will polish us with cloths of circumstance and restore what was lost. The beauty of this is that our new "shine" will have greater impact and purpose because His touch in our lives reflects His splendor.

Today, we look at life as it is. The changes that have come may have slammed into you with Category 4 hurricane strength, winds beating you to the ground. Or the new elements brought on by grief or a life change may have wrought a slower, softer, more controlled impact on your life. Either way, change has appeared, and things are not as they once were. But what does it look like? Are there words to describe your life now?

The thing I've learned from the changes I've faced in my life is that often you can do nothing but stare at it and find a place for it inside yourself. It takes some rearranging and often moving pieces of yourself around.

Both joys and heartbreak spur growth. Our joys create a sweet fragrance of gratitude. Heartbreak is God's opportunity to whisper our name so only we can hear it. He is never closer than when our breath depends on His. I don't believe God causes suffering or loss in our lives, but He for sure uses these times to make Himself known. We can withstand mighty winds of change when God stands in front of us to shelter and protect as only He can.

Remember,

"God is our refuge and strength, a very present help in trouble."

Psalm 46:1, New King James Version

PROMPTS 5-8

PROMPT 5

Let's write.

Imagine standing outside your life looking in; what would you see? Would it look broken, melted, or unstoppable? Are parts missing? Is there new building going on? Are your feet stuck in the sand, or are you wearing boots that are laced up, ready to start a new journey?

In describing life as you see it, is there any indication that God is nearby? Do you sense His presence in the circumstances, the way things developed? Just because there might not be an explanation or reason we can understand now, is there a chance God knows about it?

 *Any change, even a change for the better, is always accompanied by drawbacks and discomforts.*

~ Arnold Bennett

PROMPT 6

Let's write.

Every journey begins with a first step. We have the ability to decide. Is today "day one" for a new beginning?

Or will you postpone your new beginning and say, "One day maybe… I'll start it later"? Describe why and how you made this choice.

 *One day or day one. You decide.*

~ Unknown

PROMPT 7

Let's write.

Think about something you would like to change in yourself, in a circumstance, or in an attitude.

Take a long look and describe it in as much detail as possible. Is it time to do something about it?

 *Not everything that is faced can be changed, but nothing can be changed until it is faced.*

~ James Baldwin

PROMPT 8

Let's write.

Attitude is a powerful tool that we can control. Describe a circumstance or difficulty that comes to mind.

Now take the opposite view or imagine the "other side of the coin" and describe that. Do you have new insight?

Change the way you look at things and the things you look at change.

~ Wayne Dyer

DAY 3: REVISITING CHANGE

Grief has many layers, and I became a master at gluing them together with the heartache in my life. It took a long time to let myself experience each piece of my broken heart and let go of the hurt and disappointment.

In many ways, I'm still fighting the sadness caused by the death of my son and my husband. The trek I took through cancer brought new uncertainty.

A LIFETIME OF CHANGES

Grief often follows us for a lifetime. There is no escaping the rocky trail that follows our steps to the new place. Traveling through hard seasons takes time, perseverance, and courage. It's exhausting to keep going, especially when the road ahead is foggy and unknown. A shattered heart feels heavy and seems to take up a larger space inside the chest. The weight of our silent burden presses into cracks no one can see. Grief is a solitary journey.

It has many faces. Loss of any kind can pour the hot liquid of a broken heart into us. It finds its way inside and often has a hard time getting out. The losses that have brought life change and heartache are real and heavy. It screams out in a silence, no one hears but our own ears.

Don't be afraid of grief. It is the lava flow of healing. It's hot and burns all the places it touches, but it's necessary. Not accepting it only makes the power of grief more destructive to the new life that must come because of it. Somehow, there is a commanding strength that arises from brokenness. We learn deep truths about life and ourselves in the journey through grief. It sifts us.

When making a cake, the flour is softly spooned into a measuring cup and leveled off by scraping across the top with the back of a knife. For the texture of the end product to be excellent, the flour is dumped into a kitchen tool called a sieve. Tiny holes in the mesh strainer allow the flour to separate further, removing lumps that can cause tough pastry. Life has a way of sifting us as we are shaken through the sieve of difficulty. It has a way of refining us, changing how we see the world. For me, the losses in my life have given me a more tender eye and heart to see the pain in someone else's life. I can see it, because I have lived with the ache of grief.

 *Grief does not change you, Hazel, it reveals you.*

~ John Green

PROMPTS 9-12

PROMPT 9

Let's write.

Today is a day to write about the grief or life change in your heart. Be spontaneous and let the grief flow from the top of your head and the bottom of your heart.

Finish this sentence and keep writing for as long as you need.

Today, grief and change in my life are…

Her absence is like the sky, spread over everything.

~ C.S. Lewis, *A Grief Observed*

PROMPT 10

Let's write.

Close your eyes and imagine the "bags of cement" that are on your shoulders today. What are you carrying?

Describe it and let your words lighten the load.

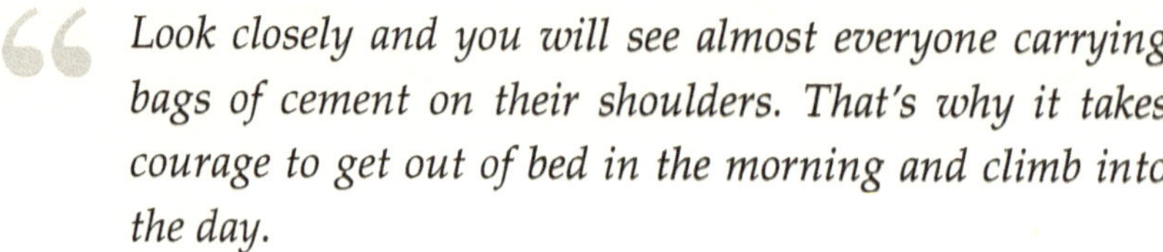

> *Look closely and you will see almost everyone carrying bags of cement on their shoulders. That's why it takes courage to get out of bed in the morning and climb into the day.*
>
> ~ Edward Hirsch

PROMPT 11

Let's write.

Fear is gripping. Grief is gripping. Both can grasp around your neck and heart and not let go.

Today, write about a time your grief felt like fear. Let the words fill the page, giving them room to evaporate.

> *No one ever told me that grief felt so like fear.*
>
> ~ C.S. Lewis

PROMPT 12

Let's write.

Memory is a healing hand. Sit in a quiet place. Take a few deep, slow breaths to relax your mind. There can be joy found in the act of remembering "the good times."

List as many of these memories as you can.

 *She was no longer wrestling with the grief, but could sit down with it as a lasting companion and make it a sharer in her thoughts.*

~ George Eliot

DAY 4: LISTENING FOR CHANGE

Today's exercise is one that makes the most difference. If you can, close your eyes and relive a situation that changed your life. You have already identified a few. Pick one, and if possible, the hardest one.

It's best to do this exercise in a quiet place where you won't be disturbed. Sitting in a comfortable chair, relaxed, works best. When I've done this, I must focus my thoughts and keep them in the place I'm going. My mind wanders, and I'm easily distracted. If you are working on *Write Your Way Through Change* in a small group setting, separate yourselves and give each other a bit of alone time to avoid feeling uncomfortable or ill at ease.

THE ASSIGNMENT IS THIS: REMEMBER. BE STILL. LISTEN. WRITE IT OUT.

Sit for as long as you like, no matter how hard, inside your chosen circumstance. If tears come or anger rises, let it happen.

The point is to let your memory guide you as you travel into that place. We're going there for a reason.

In this still place, start a dialogue with God. If you don't feel you know Him as someone to talk to, start here. Ask Him to make Himself real to you in this moment, and He will. He longs to draw you near to His side and place you in the palm of His hand. Ask Him to, and He will. Then listen for His voice.

 *"Call to me and I will answer you and tell you great and unsearchable things you do not know."*

Jeremiah 33:3 (New International Version)

God is not reluctant to speak to us if we call out to Him. He speaks because He loves us.

It may come as a thought, a sense of something new or different. His voice may be just a washing of peace that fills you as never before. God is real, and He longs for you to know it.

I discovered that truth for myself when I was 16. I asked God if he was real or not. He proved himself to be a God who loved me and knew me. I heard Him ask me why I was running away from the tug He was pulling on my heart. I asked to know him, personally, and that changed everything. I was instantly filled with peace and understanding that is nothing short of a miracle. My life has never been the same since. A simple prayer was my saving grace. If you have any questions about this, contact me through my website. 'll be happy to talk more about it. (https:// jhaney.com)

If you already have a relationship with Him, start here. Ask God to show you what He longs for you to know about the situation you have chosen to sit inside.

Is there disappointment? Are there hurt feelings? Are you angry or overwhelmed? Are you just sad? It's O.K. to feel these emotions and tell God about them. He can handle whatever you throw at Him.

God isn't required to give answers or explanations, but will offer an inner peace that can sustain you through whatever life throws your way.

In my life, there was no reason a nine-year-old boy full of life and love should wake up in heaven. I have no answer for that. My faith has grown through these circumstances, leading me to truly believe I can wait to know the reason until I see my little one again. It sounds like an excuse, but in my heart of hearts, I'm at peace with that. It doesn't mean I don't miss him or that I don't continue to feel the hole of his absence in my life, but I've been given the grace to wait.

Whatever change you're facing now, or change you're learning to live with, the key is not to feel as if God has left you. He has not.

PROMPTS 13-16

PROMPT 13

Let's write.

Today, write a letter to God about your current situation. He's our Heavenly Father and wants to hear from you. Tell Him if you are struggling and about any pain, fear, or remorse you feel, or whatever is on your mind today.

If God isn't who you are comfortable writing to, pick a person who would like to share the place you find yourself now. This isn't a letter to send, unless you want to. This writing is a telling, a sharing, and a place to ask for what you need.

Give it a try.

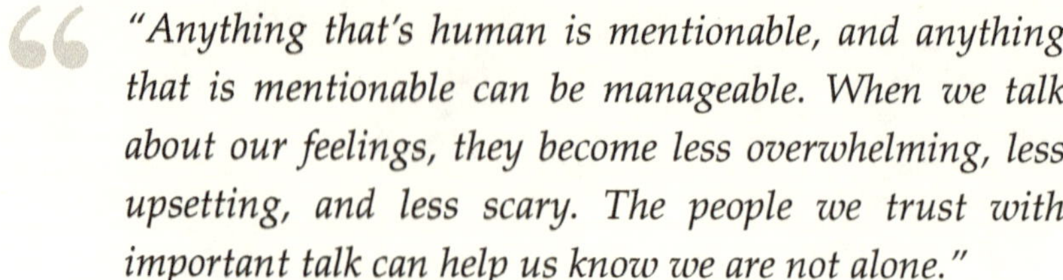

"Anything that's human is mentionable, and anything that is mentionable can be manageable. When we talk about our feelings, they become less overwhelming, less upsetting, and less scary. The people we trust with important talk can help us know we are not alone."

~ Fred Rogers

PROMPT 14

Let's write.

Hurricanes bring destruction. Change, especially unwanted change, can disrupt everything.

What's been caught inside the whirlwind that has blown your way? When things settle, what pieces can you salvage? What can be tossed to make room for something new? Describe it.

Sometimes the winds of Change are a hurricane.

~ Derek Sivers

PROMPT 15

Let's write.

Sometimes change feels like a weather front without warning. Think of a time when a change happened suddenly to you.

Now write about that change in the form of a weather forecast script to prepare someone else who might need the warning you wish you had received.

Finish the following sentence and keep writing:

Today's forecast is partly sunny with a chance of…

> *Change is hard at first, messy in the middle and gorgeous at the end.*
>
> ~ Unknown

PROMPT 16

Let's write.

Change is often built on the unknown. The familiar is comfortable, no matter how scratchy.

Describe a time when you 'fought the old' to make way for "building the new." If needed, use your five senses to spark greater detail.

> *The secret of change is to focus all of your energy, not on fighting the old, but on building the new.*
>
> ~ Socrates (Dan Millman, *Way of the Peaceful Warrior*)

DAY 5: YOUR STORY OF CHANGE

God has a distinct purpose for each of us and, if we let Him, He will use every sorrow and tear from our lives. The grief in my life is often a springboard to touch someone else's heart. They see I've learned how to live a life after losing a son, a husband, a bout with cancer, and a daughter moving away. Everyone has a story; these stories just happen to be mine. It's not harder than the struggles you face, but somehow, when we survive difficult trials, we become an example to those traveling behind us on the journey.

Your story is uniquely yours. It cries out for telling, even if it's told only to you. You at least need to hear it. But, I'll guarantee the power of it is just what someone else needs to hear.

God is in the business of restoration.

He wants to take our broken and disappointed places and use them to make us stronger. He will knit us together with others who are hurting in similar spots. Look for them.

WE NEED EACH OTHER.

What is it about telling our "story" that is so powerful? Sharing helps soften the sharp edges of anger, misfortune, or sadness that can get trapped inside a circumstance.

Giving a voice and allowing another person to hear our pain and struggles through a story opens us to the possibility of new discovery.

Jesus was a master storyteller. It was his favorite way to speak to a crowd, and he used it often. A story can touch a listener's heart and emotions in a compelling way. As events are chained together, a word picture is painted that goes somewhere.

A story carries a listener along and opens doorways of understanding or truth for both parties. Then a beam of light can shine into our hearts and give us the courage to do what we must: change.

Shaking a bottle of soda will eventually build up enough pressure for the contents to scream out, blowing the bottle cap off into a foamy mess.

Opening the lid properly to pour a glass of the bubbly liquid into an ice-filled glass is a refreshing joy. It's the same liquid, different execution.

A DRINK FOR YOUR SOUL

Sharing the hard places inside can be like twisting the plastic cap one small turn, allowing the pressure in the soft drink to escape, avoiding a volcano of angry drink bursting down the sides of the bottle.

Telling your story can be a needed release and a tall, cool drink for your soul.

PROMPTS 17-20

PROMPT 17

Let's write.

In your story of change, using the metaphor of water, did you feel as if you were "pushed out of the boat" of your life? Or did you choose to dive into these new waters? What is that water like? Is your story of change stormy? or dark, deep, scary?

Metaphorically, did you know how to swim? Did you look for the ladder to climb back on board? Did you call for help? How did it feel to find yourself in an unexpected place?

Write about what you did when your story of change struck your life and the actions you took.

Tell that story.

 *what didn't you do to bury me*

but you forgot that I was a seed

~ Dinos Christianopoulos

PROMPT 18

Let's write.

Our past is where we've come from, our future is where we're going.

How do you merge these two lanes and create a moment for today? Give examples from your own journey.

 *Life can only be understood backwards; but it must be lived forwards.*

~ Soren Kierkegaard

PROMPT 19

Let's write.

No one is exempt from hard times in life. Often, things don't work out as we wish. The question is always, what to do about it?

Write about a time when you were given the opportunity to accept a difficulty and make the best of it.

Did you "play a poor hand well?" How did you do it?

 *Life is not a matter of holding good cards, but some-times, playing a poor hand well.*

~ Jack London

PROMPT 20

Let's write.

Don't miss the opportunity of what God wants to teach you during a challenging season. Think of a difficulty that seemed to overwhelm you.

Looking back, did you discover any new possibilities? Was anything new revealed? Describe it.

 *In the middle of a difficulty lies opportunity.*

~ Albert Einstein

DAY 6: ADJUSTING TO CHANGE

If we don't adjust to the changes that come our way in life, we're sunk. There's no way to avoid the give and take: the altering of our way or the adaptation that comes from accepting the adjustment change demands. If you are like me, change is hard. Especially when a situation isn't the best, change often seems too overwhelming, and I prefer to float along in my inner tube of sameness.

Then, out of nowhere, change hits me in the face, coming around the corner, with a hidden sucker punch to the stomach, out of my control. Change rushes in with a vengeance, takes hold, and doesn't let go. The teeth of this kind of change bite deeply, leaving puncture wounds that require the attention of others. This kind of change changes everything.

It was a Monday morning, like no other. My husband jumped out of bed to wake our nine-year-old son. I was surprised by his sudden swiftness as he bolted from our room down the hallway. It was as if he had a secret whisper to discover what would change our lives forever. Especially since it was not his routine to wake the kids for school. I heard my husband's anguished scream, "He's gone!" And everything changed. My son, Mark, had passed away in his sleep.

So, what do we do when life as we know it doesn't look the same? There are many examples: a spouse leaves you for another person, a job ends before we're ready, a dream never comes true, we think it's too late to start over, illness hits us, or the death of a dear one comes too soon. Add your own trial; the list of unwanted life changes is endless. It's part of life. We have two choices: to bend or to break.

ARE YOU A PALM TREE?

A strange phenomenon was discovered during Cyclone Klaus in France in 2009. At a wind speed of 94 miles per hour, all trees broke, no matter their size, diameter, or height. They all broke. This left scientists figuring out the reason, small or skinny, large and sturdy, all trees have their breaking point. Except for one variety, the palm tree.

The palm tree has two factors in its favor: standing tall and deep roots. The fact that it bends to the powerful winds of adversity and doesn't try to resist keeps it a favorite landscape choice in tropical settings. We can learn a lot from these trees.

When life-hurricanes hit us, no matter the category of strength, if we can stand tall and bend into the grief or heartbreak, keeping watch of the friend and family roots that sustain us, we can face the destructive winds and blinding rain life throws our way. But most importantly, remember, God is watching your scene unfold, no matter how devastating. He promises to walk with us through our heartbreak and gives us the ability to bend without breaking. Alone, the winds of life can snap us in half, but with God inside the circumstance with us, we adapt. He shows us how.

LOOKING AT CIRCUMSTANCES

The key to adjusting to life changes or grief is to bend. Bending takes flexibility and practice. The stretch to find our new way takes time. We must allow ourselves to be equipped with love and care from those who surround us, including God. The weight of pain many circumstances carry is enough to easily break us, no matter the diameter of our inner strength. But, bending is best. Bending isn't easy; we can be angry or scream out in frustration at the effort it takes to move in a way we're not accustomed to. God honors bending, especially when we bend to our knees and in honest clarity call out for His helping arm.

If the hard times in your life have caused you to break, don't be discouraged. Breaking during a life-storm doesn't mean you're not strong. There are wind speeds in some circumstances that can't be tolerated, and we react as only we can. Breaking, whatever that implies to you, isn't an ending. New shoots of growth always find a place to emerge, and new beginnings can start any time along the way. We're not all made of palm trees. How terrible to never have a fall brilliance or apples. Take heart.

I've been bent to my breaking point, but just before I snapped in two, my faith took hold, and I realized God was standing right next to me. There's a saying that God won't give you more than you can handle. I don't believe that. I've been given more than I could handle. The truth to that saying is this: God will equip you to handle what you are going through. When we are equipped, we change.

A scripture to remember,

 "He only is my rock and my salvation, he is my fortress; I shall not be shaken."

Psalm 62:6 (New International Version)

PROMPT 21

Let's write.

In storms of life, are you one who can take only so much, then break? How so? Do you break in half or just lose a few "branches?" Where does your strength come from when a storm hits?

Do you see yourself bending to the winds of circumstance? If yes, how so? Have you ever prayed about the issues that bend you the most?

If yes, what was the outcome? If not, would you ever consider it?

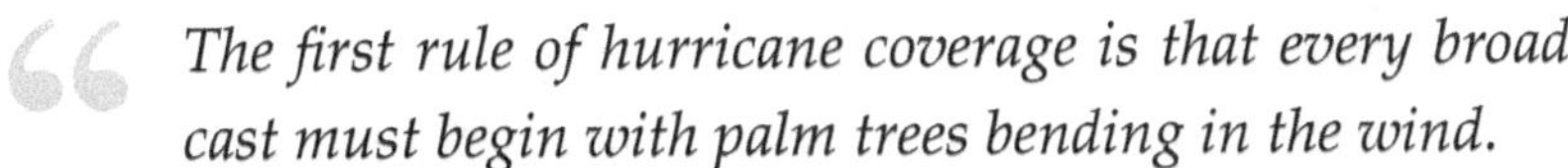

The first rule of hurricane coverage is that every broadcast must begin with palm trees bending in the wind.

~ Carl Hiaasen

PROMPT 22

Let's write.

Life is full of hills and valleys and an occasional meadow. Even the treacherous mountains we must climb have a purpose if we look for it.

What have you discovered about how to live your life well from the trials and pitfalls you have traveled?

Write about it.

The trick in life is learning how to deal with it.

~ Helen Mirren

PROMPT 23

Let's write.

Grief must be seen as a tunnel to pass through and not a cave to be trapped in. No matter the difficulty or change you're facing, head towards the light. That always points the way out.

Can you think of a time in your life when you felt trapped in the middle of a circumstance that seemed to have no way of escape?

Write about how you made it through to the other side.

The only way out is through.

~ Robert Frost

PROMPT 24

Let's write.

We've all felt defeated or overwhelmed at some point. Life is full of disappointments and crushing circumstances. These days define us. We stay broken or become champions and rise up to face the difficulty.

Think about a time when you were beaten down by life. What was your response? Were you initially battered, but took on the challenge? Or was the burden too heavy to carry, and you threw it over your shoulder for another day? Write about it.

 *Being defeated is often a temporary condition. Giving up is what makes it permanent.*

~ Marilyn vos Savant

DAY 7: CONNECTING THROUGH CHANGE

The word *connect* is vital to our survival. There is no way we could sustain ourselves without the benefit of connection to other people, places, or things. In terms of all of humankind, we need each other. We need the products and services that other people and nations provide. But most of all, we need the relationship connection between the people who happen to intersect with our lives. As the saying goes, by John Dunne, "no man is an island."

So, why is it that when life comes crashing down for whatever reason, it's so easy to isolate ourselves? I do that. I pull in all my sails and anchor my ship far from people. I want to become the island where no man is to be. It takes me a while to float through a situation and figure out how to manage or change it.

I'm not one who thinks quickly on my feet; I might come up with a perfect response hours later. We are all wired differently, and there's no right or wrong way to handle hard situations.

Personally, I connect with circumstances more slowly, and I know there are others like me.

CONNECTIONS

There are many gems in the treasure chest, and they are all valuable. There are many factors that go into the recipe for our emotional batter. I'm thankful we're not all alike!

However, the connections we have to other people are critical for our nourishment and survival. Any life-altering change throws everything into a spin, where the only way to land is to plant your feet in the ground where you find yourself and stand up. The scenery may look different, the furniture rearranged, and you may feel a little lightheaded. But your new reality is just that, new and a reality.

Give yourself time to explore the new rooms and hallways that are your life now. When losses piled up against me, I backed myself into a corner and was afraid to come out. I didn't want to be a widow, and accepting the hole my son left in my heart was choking me. It took a long time to catch my breath. So, give yourself time and space to pick up the broken-down walls to build new circles.

A major life change or grief can rock our world. You know that, or you wouldn't be working on this devotional journal.

My little boy had special needs. The day after he died, I never again saw the therapists who had become our universe for many years. After the death of my husband, my entrance into well-established social circles dried up. I was forced to make a new way socially, on my own. My connections changed. Maybe yours are changing too?

One of the most important things we can do is keep reaching out to others. It may not be the same "others" we had before our life-altering transition, but a new season grows new blooms. That's a blessing to us. As life tumbles forward after a devastating event, we learn new strategies and designs to reshape the circles broken by loss. Circles can be repaired and made stronger even when they crumble.

During seasons of life change, the soil of our lives is plowed up and eventually becomes ready for new seeds. That box is full of opportunities to reach out and help your circle heal through new relationships.

PROMPTS 25-28

PROMPT 25

Let's write.

Thinking about the connections in your life, pick one that stands beside you now and describe it as if it were a character in a book or movie. A character sketch is a journaling technique using a written description.

What do they look like? How has the person you decided to write about helped you? What kind of clothes do they wear? What is their overall demeanor? Do they have a challenge in life? Are they a sidekick or a supporting actress? Are they young or old?

Close your eyes, take a deep breath…

 *The two most important days in your life are the day you were born, and the day you find out why.*

~ Mark Twain

PROMPT 26

Let's write.

There is a way to be victorious in life, and it doesn't involve winning. Winning is a temporary, fleeting triumph. To come alongside another person and champion them, to support them and love them, is a greater victory.

Is there someone in your life who has championed you? Is there someone in your life you are the champion for? Describe and write about it.

 *When you come to look back on all that you have done in life, you will get more satisfaction from the pleasure you brought to other people's lives than you will from the times that you outdid and defeated them.*

~ Harold Kushner

PROMPT 27

Let's write.

We all have the ability to touch other people's lives. Our words have power; they can build up and encourage, or destroy and have a negative impact for a lifetime. Scripture tells us there's power in the tongue,

 *"The one who guards his mouth and tongue keeps himself out of trouble."*

Proverbs 21:23 (HCSB)

You can say you're sorry for words spoken in anger or hate, but you can never take them back.

Do you remember a time you spoke words you wish you could take back?

What were the circumstances and the outcome?

 *Open, honest communication is the best foundation for any relationship, but remember that at the end of the day it's not what you say or what you do, but how you make people feel that matters most.*

~ Tony Hsieh, *Delivering Happiness*

PROMPT 28

Let's write.

We all have times when we feel vulnerable and fragile. It takes courage to be brave. There is risk in exposing our feelings or taking the first step towards something new.

Which side of the above quote have you experienced: taking a hand to begin a journey, or allowing someone to take yours?

Both have the same outcome. You must be fearless.

Describe your experience.

Sometimes, reaching out and taking someone's hand is the beginning of a journey. At other times, it is allowing another to take yours.

~ Vera Nazarian, The Perpetual Calendar of Inspiration

WEEK TWO

"Some changes look negative on the surface, but you will soon realize that space is being created in your life for something new to emerge."

~ Eckhart Tolle

CHANGE BRINGS

Change is expected, necessary, and part of the process of living. We need change to survive. Our seasons are designed to give us times of planting, growing, and harvest. It's easy to see how missing a single step in the process can damage the harvest.

I'm not a farmer, but I know that if the seed is old or damaged, the plant will suffer. The growing season has a marked number of days for the proper bloom to appear. Picking fruit before it's ready makes for crunchy peaches. The design is unique to each species, including us.

There is a timing mechanism instilled in life that keeps order and the growth process moving forward. I'm glad I don't have the insight of a fifteen-year-old in my sixties. I have wisdom and understanding that come only from living a long life, and my life is unique to me. That sounds obvious, and it is, but we need to remember even those who share our lives aren't exactly like us on the inside. We can share the same circle with others, but in the end, we stand alone to face what life throws at us and can choose how we will react.

Life transitions have many components. There is the unfamiliar, the unknown, an unseen aspect, and often, change is something unwanted. It causes us to feel unprepared. Each of these layers will be highlighted below, along with exercises to help you see how the changes in your life are important parts of who you are.

We are marked by change: it has etched each of us in a unique and dynamic way. Take the time to explore your life and to embrace the changes now and in the future.

Life is a gift.

DAY 8: CHANGE BRINGS THE UNFAMILIAR

Especially now that I find myself alone, I feel uncomfortable, out of my comfort zone in an unfamiliar setting. I don't know why having another person at my side gives me the courage to face new things. If I have a friend with me, I can walk into a party full of strangers, strike up a conversation, and enjoy the evening. Face that same group alone, I hug the perimeter of the room, feeling invisible, and I usually leave early.

COURAGE FOR THE UNFAMILIAR

We often have to do things we don't want to do or don't feel especially self-confident about. Truth be told, I dislike new things.

However, years ago, with no knowledge or understanding, I opened a knitting shop. The small shop was a delight to the eye, with yarns from around the world packed into black shelving bins. I had no idea how to run a business. I had zero confidence and no grasp of what I was getting myself into. Even so, I opened the door to entrepreneurship and walked through.

Almost two decades later, the shop is still a place of community. It's a unique setting where lasting friendships are made, not to mention lovely knit things! Learning to run a small retail business was scary, but as the years progressed, it filled me with bravery. The help I needed appeared: skilled staff, a knowledgeable bookkeeper, and customers who would become family.

I tell that story to encourage you not to wait, if a prompting is laid inside your heart to do something or talk to someone, do it! Take the chance and the steps to do that thing. It might just change everything.

When we're full of grief or heartbreak, or lack understanding, a broken spirit can quickly talk us out of what might be our destiny. Just because a thing is unfamiliar doesn't mean it's not for you. That is just the place God wants us to be, so He can show up and demonstrate His strength poured into us. Live long enough, and you will encounter things that are "too much to bear." That's when God strides in and helps shoulder the load, if we ask Him.

Whatever you've gone through or are living with now, no matter how unfamiliar it seems, there's a plan for this thing to mold you into a stronger person. And that's just what God desires for us. There's a seat at the table with your name on it, a banquet of new things.

SPEAKING YOUR NEEDS

It's easy to wear a mask of well-being when inside, but we're full of hurt and deep disappointment. I became a master of keeping the storm of loss tucked away from view. As the years progressed, I learned how to walk around the holes and losses left inside me.

There were days when I would sit at the edge of the cavern and let my feet dangle into the space once filled by my son and husband. I didn't understand why they had to die so young and leave me as the one to stay behind. I was forced to pick up the pieces of my shattered life. The shards were sharp and often cut my heart, but it was a job only I could do. Or so I thought.

Once I decided I needed more than I could give myself, and had the courage to share my suffering, the scaffolding of other people's arms came around me. It was like an Amish barn raising, where the community I forgot was mine showed up with the necessary equipment to help me stand up. They built what I needed, listened when I needed to cry out, and brought the nourishment of love and acceptance. My new state was new to me, and they helped me find my way.

 *"Where two or more are gathered in my name, there am I with them."*

Matthew 18:20 (New International Version)

Often, people don't pray specifically for us because they don't know our needs.

If you are praying about something alone, don't feel that God doesn't hear you. He wants us to gather other people around to share what's on our hearts and minds.

WE NEED EACH OTHER

Your unfamiliar situation becomes familiar at the feet of the one who knows all about you and will not leave you alone on the journey. The Bible reminds us to,

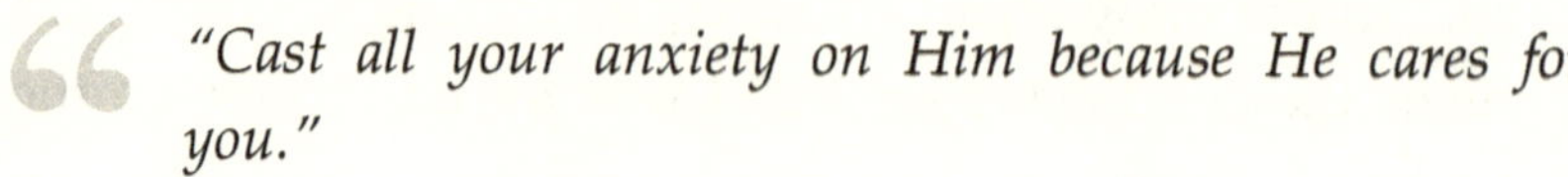

"Cast all your anxiety on Him because He cares for you."

1 Peter 5:7 (New International Version)

Let the people in your life care for you, too.

PROMPTS 29-32

PROMPT 29

Let's write.

Are there situations or settings that cause you to feel uncomfortable or unsure of yourself? Why do you think these situations bring discomfort? Do you avoid these settings or soldier through, making the best of it? Is there something you feel unfamiliar with doing, or a place to go that feels unknown, that your heart is telling you, 'now is the time'? If you feel unsure or held back, what's keeping you from taking the steps toward that thing or asking for help?

What is your action plan to take the steps necessary to do the unfamiliar thing? No matter how small, list some steps to get started. Do you have prayer requests for your unfamiliar situation? Can you lay them at the feet of heaven and release your fear or anxiety in trying it or moving forward? Do you have loved ones or friends you can ask to come alongside you?

 *Man cannot discover new oceans unless he has the courage to lose sight of the shore.*

~ Andre Gide

PROMPT 30

Let's write.

Do you think your hard times have shaped who you are today? Do accumulated difficulties lead to wisdom?

How so? Or why not?

 *Even the hard times are part of your life story. If you acknowledge them and move past them, they eventually add up to the experiences that make you wise.*

~ Miley Cyrus

PROMPT 31

Let's write.

Every story has a beginning, middle, and an ending. In between, the pages make chapters that put a story into perspective. Think of a season in your life that can be remembered in story form.

Where does the start take place? What happened in the middle of the circumstance? What was the resolution or ending? Did you discover any surprises in your written version?

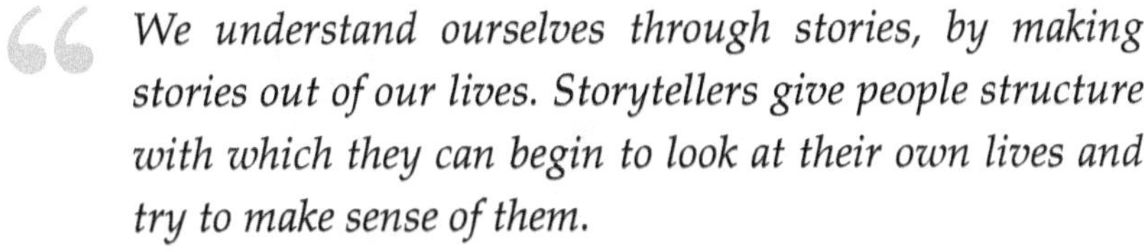

We understand ourselves through stories, by making stories out of our lives. Storytellers give people structure with which they can begin to look at their own lives and try to make sense of them.

~ Bill Harley

PROMPT 32

Let's write.

If your life were a movie, would you be the actor, writer, director, set designer, or audience?

Explain why...

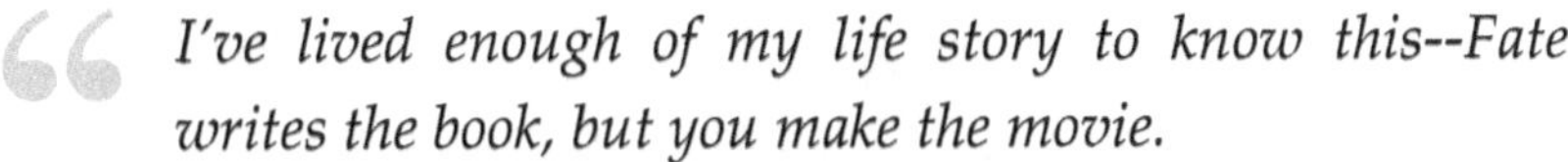

I've lived enough of my life story to know this--Fate writes the book, but you make the movie.

~ Robert Breault

DAY 9: CHANGE BRINGS THE UNKNOWN

There is no way to plan for the unknown.

When my husband died, my life took a drastic turn toward the unknown. We were married for twenty-six years and dated for five. He was a steady influence in my life. I was widowed at age fifty-five. I wasn't prepared to be pushed off the path my life was taking. With one hard shove, I found myself rolling down a hill that had no end in sight.

My husband's cancer battle lasted many years; I always thought he would beat it. Even at his sickest, I was sure God would use a miraculous healing as a powerful testimony for others to witness God's grace.

It didn't work out that way. When all the funeral formalities were over, and everyone went back to the life they knew, I stepped into my new reality. This was unknown, uncharted territory for me. I was scared. had entered a new land.

All at once, everything changed, and I was thrust into a dimension I couldn't prepare for. I felt as if I woke up in another country. I didn't understand the customs and routine of this foreign place of widowhood. The language was new, and I was not given the manual. I looked the same on the outside, but the inside felt weak and empty.

No matter the life change that has dropped into your life, there's the unknown attached to it. We can't know something until it happens, and even then, it must unfold. We can imagine, dream, or wonder, but to step into a new place or to pick up a new thing, there is uncertainty. Discovery and clarification will come, eventually.

THE NEW LAND

 *"But I trust in you, O Lord; I say, 'You are my God.' My times are in your hands…"*

Psalm 31:14-15 (New International Version)

Knowing my times were in God's hands, even the unknown times, made all the difference. I was devastated and in grief, but felt the framework of my faith in an unseen God holding me up. I knew He was in my circumstance, shining a light on my feet, showing me I had the courage to keep going, because I wasn't alone.

I traveled those dark days often with my eyes shut, not wanting to face the reality that my husband was no longer in my life. He filled in the parts of me that were not enough.

However, long before my husband's cancer took deep hold, I remember praying hard that God would "just heal him!" I'll never forget God's breath in my ear speaking to me, asking, "Why aren't I enough?"

Years later, when I needed someone to be more than enough in my life, those words came flooding back to my mind. God proved himself to be that one.

He knows our unknown. Our future is His yesterday. Trust Him for that.

PROMPTS 33-36

PROMPT 33

Let's write.

When you feel broken and in pieces, empty of what it takes to keep going, is there someone you cry out to? Even a silent cry can thunder in God's ear.

What would you say to God if you cried out to Him in this new, unknown land?

 *"A diamond is a chunk of coal that did well under pressure."*

~ Henry Kissinger

Prompt 34

Let's write.

Hope rises from darkness. Light, no matter how faint, can seep in under a doorway of circumstance and change everything.

Think of a dark night in your life, and describe how the sunrise of another day helped you keep going.

Even the darkest nights will end and the sun will rise.

~ Unknown

Prompt 35

Let's write.

Mindset makes all the difference. Our perspective can reverse the truth into a falsehood.

Do you agree? Write about a circumstance that was difficult to adjust to. Were you a "wise person?" Or a "fool" adjusting the truth to suit your thinking? Describe what happened.

When truth presents itself, the wise person sees the light, takes it in, and makes adjustments. The fool tries to adjust the truth so he does not have to adjust to it.

~ Henry Cloud

PROMPT 36

Let's write.

Worry is made of fabric that can scratch and feel uncomfortable, or fill your soul and drown you. Have you had a time where worry took over and depleted your strength?

What was the outcome? Write about it.

 "Worry does not empty tomorrow of its troubles. It empties today of its strength."

~ Corrie Ten Boom

DAY 10: CHANGE BRINGS THE UNSEEN

I wish I had better eyesight. I've been wearing glasses since the third grade.

I remember squinting my eyes so tightly, trying to make out the words written in white chalk. I don't know how long I struggled before I was given a pair of blue cat-eye-shaped glasses that changed everything. Suddenly, I didn't panic when the spelling words were listed on the blackboard. I could see them! Having a clear vision when math was explained brought new understanding. My grades improved, as well as my third-grade self-confidence. All of this came from improved sight.

I'll never forget, even at that young age, how remarkable it was to see things clearly at a distance, especially the blackboard.

Sharp vision is something I take for granted now, until I take my glasses off. My 20/20 vision suddenly becomes blurry, with no defined lines or shapes. Without glasses, I can hardly make out my hand in front of my face. I'll never be able to thank the person who invented spectacles enough. Glasses have been around since the thirteenth century! I would be lost without them.

Some days, I wish someone would invent a way to see life more clearly. Living my days, right before me, I still struggle to understand. Often, there is no rhyme or reason to the unfolding of circumstances over which we have no control.

The future is ours, but not promised, and perhaps that's a blessing.

WHAT'S YOUR VISION?

Scripture reminds us to live one day at a time.

> *"So, don't worry about tomorrow, for tomorrow will bring its own worries. Today's trouble is enough for today."*

Matthew 6:34 (New International Version)

We can't see tomorrow or the next hour, for that matter. It's unseen to us, regardless of what we think or how much we plan. I'm sure God designed life to be that way on purpose. He loves us too much to let us see more than we can handle. Think of the stress of having knowledge ahead of this moment. Our brains couldn't deal with the overload.

God knows that, because He made us.

It's our nature to want to know and understand. It helps us feel in control and gives our lives structure. God has wired us to be curious, and our brains have a remarkable capacity to design and solve problems. But sometimes, there is no answer to our questions.

God, in His wisdom, transformed everything when He poured faith into the mix. Grief, or any life transition, throws us into waters that feel choppy, full of white caps, and we can't feel the bottom. Looking out when there is no dry land, no solution, or an ending, fear can take over. Just know, the best way through violent seas is to press into the life vest that God provides: His peace. Flailing arms of despair and panic only lead to collapse and exhaustion.

"So, we fix our eyes not on what is seen, but on what is unseen. For what is seen is temporary, but what is unseen is eternal."

2 Corinthians 4:18 (New International Version)

Life may feel uncertain, full of blurred change ahead. Faith is the solution that clears the way. How like a loving God to make a way for us that comes only from Him. We want to see what's ahead in life, but we can't, no matter how hard we try.

God is the unseen that we can know. His gift of faith is what allows us to move in the dark, no matter how many rocks are in the way. Faith that God is walking beside us and has the map is the only way to see the unseen.

PROMPTS 37-40

PROMPT 37

Let's write.

Have you ever considered the thought that everything comes with a price? Forging through life takes a toll. We purchase good times and difficulties with our decisions, our attitude, and discipline.

Write about what comes to mind when you think about the path you currently find yourself on.

What has been the cost?

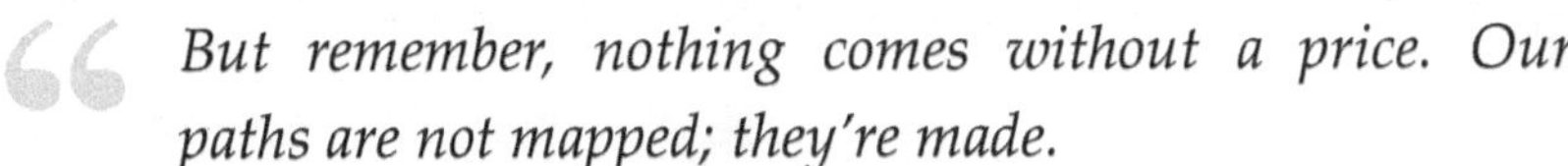

> But remember, nothing comes without a price. Our paths are not mapped; they're made.
>
> ~ Priya Ardis, *Even my Merlin*

PROMPT 38

Let's write.

A path is not always straight or flat. Often, we find ourselves out of breath, weak, and empty, trudging up a mountainside that seems to have no summit.

Write about a decision, a door you walked through, or a season in your life that changed you.

 *What you're missing is the path itself changes you.*

~ Julien Smith, *The Flinch*

PROMPT 39

Let's write.

Life is often about how we handle 'plan B.' What we thought was a certainty can come crashing around our feet, sending shards of broken dreams or promises scattered across our hearts.

What to do? Formulate Plan B. Have you ever had to step over what was and build something new? Describe it.

 *No, sometimes life beats you down. Sometimes life deserts you, and your only choice is to find another path.*

~ Rebekah Crane, *The Upside of Falling Down*

PROMPT 40

Let's write.

Describe a time when God answered a prayer of desperation in your life. Looking back, did the answer strengthen your faith to trust God for more? If so, how so?

Is there a way that 2 Corinthians 5:7, "We walk by faith, not by sight..." can apply to your situation? How so?

Today, journal any thoughts on the concept of that faith in second chances.

 *To improve is to change; to be perfect is to change often.*

~ Winston S. Churchill

DAY 11: CHANGE BRINGS THE UNWANTED

We get one chance to live each day. When it's over, it's vanished; there's no way to get it back. God designed time to be a precious gift of hours and minutes to help us mark days and keep track of years. We're the only species He gave the division of time to. It marks us. Time zooms by and can't be stopped.

There are hundreds of situations and circumstances I would love to revisit. I would spend more time with my babies and not rush to vacuum the living room. I would go fly fishing with my husband instead of staying home to run errands. I would sit next to my Dad and share watching basketball, knowing how much he loved the sport. I would crouch on the sidewalk with my son and watch the ants, as he loved to do. I would sit at the end of my daughter's bed and watch her fall asleep.

All these, such small things. Moments lost. What I would give to have five minutes back to be with those who are now gone. The time has passed on, as have they.

Life is full of the unwanted.

I never thought I would wake one morning to discover my nine-year-old son had finished his days on earth. Without a sound, he slipped into heaven. I never imagined my husband's days would be filled with pain and decline as cancer moved in and never left. I never considered that cancer would be part of my story and give me body-altering surgery. I never pictured my daughter, who has become my dear friend, would find her destiny and the love of her life so far from home.

We have certain preconceived ideas about how things in life are supposed to be, and often they don't turn out the way we planned.

PLAN B

My daughter once gave me a beautiful goblet with the words inscribed, "Life is all about Plan B." Looking at a list of Plan A's that didn't come to pass can fill you with sadness and regret. Plan B may not be where we want to go, but it's often the only road in front of us.

As time passes, a new reality will become clear. We must often grow into the place where life deposits us. It may feel unwanted and scratchy at first. It takes time to learn how to make the new garment fit. Be patient and know you're not alone, even if you find yourself standing in a corner.

For years, my reality defined me. I felt as if the word *widow* was taped across my head. It's how I saw myself, and I viewed life through that lens. It colored everything in my heart and horizon. I wore this reality like an old, baggy sweater. It was prickly and uncomfortable, hanging from my shoulders. I felt the heavy, long sleeves of a reality only I could see.

When life hits you hard, and there's nothing you can do about the unwanted change it brings, the only thing to do is look up. By that, I mean this is the time to take a serious look at your faith to discover that God is as real as He says He is. Scripture reminds us;

"Now faith is being sure of what we hope for and certain of what we do not see."

Hebrews 11:1 (New International Version)

There is a difference between knowing about God and knowing God. In measuring inches between our head and our heart, the distance is very small. In measuring faith, the distance to the heart is all that matters.

Faith in God gives a peace that comes from believing He knows all about the situation and circumstance from start to finish. It's the framework that holds our lives together when we have no power or strength to do so on our own.

A favorite quote speaks to my heart concerning faith,

"To learn strong faith is to endure great trials. I have learned my faith by standing firm amid severe trials."

~ George Mueller

George Mueller was the director of an orphanage in Bristol, England, in the 1800s. He was a Christian evangelist and cared for more than 10,000 orphans in his lifetime. He has a remarkable life story of faith for God to supply the needs of hungry and discarded children. His faith was unshakable, even in the face of unwanted circumstances, and was the fuel that burned into a passion that changed a generation.

We're never prepared for the unwanted transitions in life. They will come as sure as you are reading this sentence. The challenge is how we face unwelcome situations: with bitterness and fear, or confidence that comes from God pouring His purpose into the circumstance.

A favorite scripture verse, and one that carried me through trials in my life, is,

 *"We live by faith, not by sight."*

2 Corinthians 5:7 (New International Version)

This verse is etched into my heart; I know I don't have to see to have faith.

God loves it when we are honest with our feelings and desires. He doesn't get mad or punish us for coming to Him with our hearts heavy or disappointed or even mad.

This verse says it all,

 *"Come to me, all you who are weary and burdened and I will give you rest."*

Matthew 11:28 (New International Version)

That's a promise. God keeps all promises, even if not on our timeline and even if we can't see it.

PROMPTS 41-44

Prompt 41

Let's write.

Are there things in your life that haven't turned out as you expected? List a few.

Are there parts of your life now that seem like a Plan B? Describe them.

How do you see yourself in the new reality of your life? Is there a reality you are living that colors the way you view life?

Is there a term or phrase that describes that place, even if it's only in your mind or heart? If you can, describe it.

 *Part broken- part whole, you begin again.*

~ Jeanette Winterson

PROMPT 42

Let's write.

Bravery is made, not bought. It's forged from fear, worry, and anxiety. The result of stepping out into the unknown of a situation or decision that brings distress is the wonderful realization that you did what you were afraid to do.

Has this ever happened to you? Describe the discovery you made about yourself.

> *One of the greatest discoveries a person makes, one of their great surprises, is to find they can do what they were afraid they couldn't do.*
>
> ~ Henry Ford

PROMPT 43

Let's write.

There are two sides to water. It's completely necessary for our survival, yet it can bring horrific destruction from a storm or a broken bathroom pipe.

Sometimes the "new waters" can feel as out of control as a hurricane, or as refreshing as a tall glass filled with ice water and lemon. Either way, life presents us with circumstances we must step into.

Describe a time when you entered new waters. Did you encounter a storm or calm, restful waters? Write about it.

 *Enter new waters.*

~ Robert Green

PROMPT 44

Let's write.

"Old ways" are often safe ways. We're creatures of habit and comfort and can resist a new way. However, old keys don't open new locks.

Do you have an example of resisting a new thing, not wanting to let go of the old way?

Write about it. What was the struggle?

 *Old ways won't open new doors.*

~ Unknown

DAY 12: CHANGE BRINGS THE UNPREPARED

Being prepared is the groundwork for any success. Having homework done, priming the wall properly before painting a bubblegum-pink bedroom, or doing a gauge swatch before knitting a sweater (knitting lingo) are preparations for success. Foundations make for pleasing results in the end. Preparation produces: good grades, a room with no pink undertone, and a sweater that fits properly.

I've attempted many things not fully prepared; in fact, I seem to always operate more from the "wing-it" side than the "completely prepared beforehand" side of the coin. It's how I'm wired. Give me a spreadsheet of numbers and my eyes cross faster than a horse running in the Kentucky Derby! Have a fun idea pop into my head, and I'm all in, off and running. We spur-of-the-moment folks need you steady and prepared types in our lives. You're the ones who plan through to the end; we never finish anything, and appreciate your help!

My life changed completely when my husband died. He was the sturdy one, the rod that kept me grounded. Without him, I felt untethered, as if floating above my life. I wondered how I would ever sew up all the holes he left in me. He was the person who filled in places that were not big enough. My husband expanded me. He loved adventure and new things, and I was always by his side. My life was made bigger by his life and made smaller by his passing.

The years are passing, more quickly than I would like, and I've worked hard at repackaging my life with the change that surrounds it. When life-altering circumstances come, we have no choice but to jump into the thrashing waters and see where the current takes us. The beginning can be tremulous, heading downstream in the whitewater of the unknown, feeling unprepared. We're eventually dropped into a calm eddy of stillness where reality can take hold, prepared or not.

READY OR NOT

There is no way to prepare for the unknown things life throws our way. We may think we have it all wrapped up tightly held in our arms, but we don't. All it takes is a phone call about a mammogram discovery, a slippery piece of black ice on the highway on the way home, or a son who lives only 9 years to know we have no say in some of the events we face.

The key to dealing with the situations that leave us unprepared is to accept that life is bigger than we are. God designed us to withstand the hardest of days with His help. Where we go wrong is trying to stand up alone again and again when the wind is knocked out of our lungs.

God intended for us to be in community with others, but mostly to be in fellowship with Him. He will walk beside us through circumstances we're unprepared to face, because He knows them from beginning to end. We only see the moment; He sees it all. Our pain and heartbreaks are real and mark us deeply, but the grace God pours over our wounds and gives us breath to keep walking.

Here is a scripture of hope,

"God is our refuge and strength, an ever-present help in trouble."

Psalm 46:1 (New International Version)

What I love about this verse is the promise that God is not only present in our trouble, but He is a 'very present' help in trouble. That speaks to me, especially today when we expect instant results for everything. I send a text, and if I don't hear an instant response wonder if the person received it! We have fast food, instant messaging, express lanes, and drive-thru in every imaginable arena. It's a blessing to know our God is very present and always there, especially when we need Him most.

We may feel unprepared to face what's ahead, but no matter how alone we feel, we're not. God loves us and will prepare us in advance for the things we are unprepared to face.

'Trust in the LORD with all your heart and lean not on your own understanding; in all your ways submit to Him, and He will make your paths straight."

Proverbs 3:5-6 (New International Version)

When we feel the most unprepared to face a trial, God is the most prepared to help us through it.

PROMPTS 45-48

Prompt 45

Let's write.

Do you think it's possible for God to walk beside you during the hard times in your life? How? Do you have an example of a time when you knew God was helping you through a tough situation?

Are you the type of person who prepares ahead of time for things? Do you know why? Have you had a season or circumstance in your life where you felt unprepared? Did you have a specific strategy to cope with the change your circumstances opened?

Think of a circumstance that hit your life, you weren't prepared for. Did it send your life in a new direction? Write about it.

 *"What's happened to me, he thought. It was no dream."*

~ Franz Kafka

PROMPT 46

Let's write.

What do you think the above quote is talking about? What kind of gifts can change bring?

Write about it. Give details from your experience.

 *Change always comes bearing gifts.*

~ Price Pritchett

PROMPT 47

Let's write.

Sitting on the dock waiting for something to be different works for a while. But time isn't always the currency for a new thing. At some point, it's up to us to make a change happen.

Can you relate to the above statement? Give your mind space to recall a time when you took hold of a situation that caused a change. What happened? Did you "swim out to meet it?"

 *If your ship doesn't come in, swim out and meet it.*

~ Jonathan Winters

PROMPT 48

Let's write.

It's easy to pile up excuses or find someone to blame for why a particular thing has or has not happened...

Being as honest as you can, write about an excuse that stopped you from doing something you wanted to do.

 *If you really want to do something, you'll find a way. If you don't, you'll find an excuse.*

~ Jim Rohn

DAY 13: CHANGE BRINGS THE UNCERTAIN

Uncertainty is a difficult place to live. Its roadway is unmarked and seems dangerous. It can house all kinds of fear, real and imagined. Life in the face of uncertainty is vague and cloudy. I know, I've been there. During each of the major life transitions and grief seasons I've experienced, I was pulled into a hole of not feeling certain about anything in my life, including me!

In these times, life can feel off balance and crooked. We don't know where to put our feet, or even where the proper shoes hide! A mist of not knowing covers all corners of life and makes even the things we know slippery and damp. I don't like this place, but it must be visited; it's part of the scenery on the grief-and-major-life-change journey.

Uncertainty is not a place to stay longer than is necessary. Until our footing is recalibrated and we discover the boots required to climb over the hill, we must make the best of the place. Not liking uncertainty makes traveling out a priority. Our new life can't move forward if we constantly slip backward into indecision or insecurity. It's dangerous here.

ENTERING UNCERTAINTY

Unpleasant as the feeling of uncertainty is, there are benefits. Standing in the middle of decisions, having both feet on each side of the fence and not knowing which way to turn, gives us a chance to consider options. The more choices we have, the more control we regain over our lives.

Indecision is a mark of grief. Somehow, our brains become swamped by deep sorrow. It's as if suffering swells and takes over our thinking and judgment. There's only so much room in our mind, and grief demands space. Time allows the hurt to be absorbed and accepted, so be patient.

I remember soon after our little boy died, my husband and I were given the task to pick a video from the local video shop for visiting family to watch. They thought it would be a help to give us a project and get us out of the house. It didn't. I'm sure I was the first person to burst into tears because I was so overwhelmed by choosing a movie to rent! We left empty-handed; the task was too enormous to complete.

Grief, no matter the cause, can short-circuit even the simplest task. Decision-making is one example. Give yourself space and time.

You may be far down the road of your change journey and have the uncertainty segment in your rear-view mirror. Confidence comes as pieces of the puzzle fall into place. Doors open to a new opportunity, ushering in something new. We learn how to live around the hole grief cuts into our lives, and a new normal starts growing. But be aware, uncertainty will always follow close behind. It stalks us and wants attention.

Life is fragile. Uncertainty, when splashed with the fuel of fear, can burst into an uncontrollable raging flame that destroys everything good in its path.

We have a promise from God that He knows the plans for us, if we have ears to hear his voice.

"I will instruct you and teach you in the way you should go; I will counsel you with my eye upon you."

Psalm 32:8 (English Standard Version)

Don't let the weight of uncertainty in your life explode and disrupt the lesson God wants you to learn. The school of sorrow has many textbooks; only God has the teacher's edition.

PROMPTS 49-52

PROMPT 49

Let's write.

Today is a day to write about uncertainty. How has it washed into your life? What does it look like? Give it a shape or a noun. Describe how uncertainty in your particular circumstance has impacted you.

Have you felt the pull into uncertainty during your grief or life change journey? How did you cope? How did it feel? And how long did you stay? Are you still in the neighborhood of uncertainty, or have you climbed out?

 *"What has been is no more. Change has come."*

~ Dean Koontz

PROMPT 50

Let's write.

Change is often hard. Changing ourselves is even harder. Seeing a situation from another point of view, or realizing pride or self-ishness has come to the forefront, is hard to admit. Even a small attitude adjustment is all it takes to shed new light on a circumstance.

Have you ever realized the power inside to choose an inner change? What did you do? What was the result? Write about a situation where you changed, and it made a difference.

 *When we are no longer able to change a situation, we are challenged to change ourselves.*

~ Viktor Frankl

PROMPT 51

Let's write.

Hindsight is always easy. Standing in the present and looking back offers a grander perspective. Options or outcomes hidden at the onset of a choice are made visible when looking back. It takes courage to step into the unknown, a path not always clearly marked.

Have you had the experience of taking a path that was unfa-miliar at the start, with results that surprised you? Write about it.

It's well and good to look back after the fact and see what we should have done, but we rarely know what path is best when we take that first step.

~ Christine Freehan, *Oceans of Fire*

PROMPT 52

Let's write.

Do you agree that our life path is not straight? Have you had an experience of getting "lost?" What was the result?

Write about the circumstance.

The path to our destination is not always a straight one. We go down the wrong road, we get lost, we turn back. Maybe it doesn't matter which road we embark on. Maybe what matters is that we embark.

~ Barbara Hall

DAY 14: CHANGE BRINGS THE UNCOMFORTABLE

Change can feel like an ill-fitting, scratchy wool sweater. You want to take it off as soon as possible and never wear it again. The effects can be felt, even after it's removed. Your skin prickles at the thought of it! Sometimes, change can feel like that, and certainly grief has a physical memory to it.

Any kind of change, positive or negative, disrupts the balance of our lives. We become accustomed to how the rooms of our lives look, and any new décor can cause imbalance. New babies disrupt our sleep, a new spouse disrupts life alone, sudden retirement removes the reason to get up in the morning, and so on.

Change in our world can't be avoided. The million-dollar question is: what do we do about changes, especially those that bring sandbags of discomfort? They are hard to wear and harder to carry around.

During the heavy grief season of loss in my life, simple activities brought me emotional discomfort. After my little boy died, it was like a knife through my heart to see his school bus on my street. Every day at 3:15, I was reminded of my loss; no one got dropped off at my house anymore. For a long time, I tried not to be home in the afternoon. It seemed silly to drive around to no place in particular, just to avoid the pain of seeing Bus 64.

All loss brings discomfort. Sometimes I still notice I'm an extra wheel when dining with my couple of friends. We adjust and get accustomed to how change has repainted the walls of our world, but it's hard not to prefer the old colors.

LOOK OUT, HERE COMES CHANGE

Discomfort has a positive side. Removing a hot baking dish from the oven will quickly teach the lesson to always use an oven mitt. I've had many experiences where my discomfort in a situation prompted me to choose a better way.

Making our way into a new place is uncomfortable. We don't know what to expect or how to manage at first. Scripture tells us,

"Do not despise these small beginnings, for the Lord rejoices to see the work begin."

Zechariah 4:10 (New Living Translation)

Small beginnings can be anything. They feel awkward and uncomfortable at first. The hesitation to embark on a new place in life, or even to change our thinking about something, takes effort but can start small. Don't underestimate the value of small steps. God loves to use small things. The story in scripture tells of how a boy's small lunch of a few fish and some loaves of bread fed over 5,000 people.

 *"Another of his disciples, Andrew, Simon Peter's brother, spoke up, 'Here is a boy with five small barley loaves and two small fish, but how far will they go among so many?' Jesus said, 'Have the people sit down.' There was plenty of grass in that place, and they sat down (about five thousand men were there). Jesus then took the loaves, gave thanks, and distributed to those who were seated as much as they wanted. He did the same with the fish."*

John 6:8-11 (New International Version)

We never know how a small step, a brave decision, or a kind word will bloom into a miraculous event. God's touch on a common situation or person can open doors to opportunities that burst with possibilities.

Don't disregard any small start or idea. Put into God's hands, anything can happen, even a change that will blow your mind! Just because the start of something new is uncomfortable doesn't mean it's not to be done. Don't wait until you aren't scared before you step out. Sometimes, being scared is the reason to step out.

A first at something will only happen once. After that, you've done that thing before.

PROMPTS 53-56

PROMPT 53

Let's write.

Has the change or grief you've experienced changed the color of the walls of your world? Have you felt uncomfortable in the change you are now accepting? What does that look like? Do you think the uncomfortable feeling you've experienced in your change has helped move you to make decisions to avoid or alter anything in your life now?

Is there anything you have done in your circumstance that was a "first" of something? Did you feel uncomfortable doing that thing? What did you do? Have you repeated that new thing now? Does it feel less uncomfortable because you've done it before? If yes, how so?

When you think about the greatness of small beginnings, what do you think of? Is it something you've already started, or something you want to begin?

Do you see any place in your world where small beginnings can make a difference? How will you start moving toward something new? Or, what was your success or uncomfortable place if you have already started a small beginning?

 *Change has to come for life to struggle forward.*

~ Helen Hollick

PROMPT 54

Let's write.

Do you have a circumstance where you found yourself in a state of "between?" Where is the "middle of nowhere" in your life? Have you been there?" Write about it.

 *Sometimes you find yourself in the middle of nowhere, and sometimes in the middle of nowhere is where you find yourself.*

~ Unknown

PROMPT 55

Let's write.

Uncertainty is a rocky place to live. It feels uncomfortable, and there's no clear path. However, uncertainty is where the future calls to us, so we can be pulled into something new.

Have you experienced a time of uncertainty that didn't make sense until later on?

Write about that.

 *Embrace uncertainty. Some of the most beautiful chapters in our lives won't have a title until much later.*

~ Bob Goff

PROMPT 56

Let's write.

Have you ever had a dream or a plan that absorbed you? What did you do about it? What was the outcome? Write about it.

 *Never give up on something that you can't go a day without thinking about.*

~ Winston Churchill

WEEK THREE

"Change happens very slow and very sudden."

~Dorothy Bryant

CHANGE MAKES

Change can hit hard. It can be unexpected and unwanted, and throw us for a loop. How we travel through the twists and turns to land on our feet in a new place takes patience and a plan. Stepping away from a familiar role, a relationship, or a routine can be like tearing apart two sheets of glued-together paper. There are spots that don't give away, leaving ripped edges behind and patches of the old.

It's a myth that change comes in smooth segments with no residue of the past. The old way no longer fits when a major life change comes knocking. Our job is to open the door and make room for something new.

There is often some rearranging that needs to be done of our habits, beliefs, and strengths. Like new furniture arriving in our homes, the old pieces get moved around or are discarded. Not letting go of unnecessary things creates clutter and robs us of the joy of enjoying new things.

DAY 15: CHANGE MAKES
NEW CHALLENGES

I'm not one for challenges. There are some who see the mountain ahead and race to climb it, no matter what. I'm the other sort; I see a challenge and wonder how to get out of it or run the other way. I'm not saying I'm a quitter, but sometimes it feels that way to me. I need time to process and talk through a circumstance, even if the conversation is only in my head.

When it comes to problems or challenges, small pieces work better for me. Viewing the big picture all at once can be too painful or just too big to accept. They ask, 'How do you eat an elephant?' The answer is one bite at a time. That's true for elephant eating and true for accepting things too hard to swallow in one bite.

Scripture tells us,

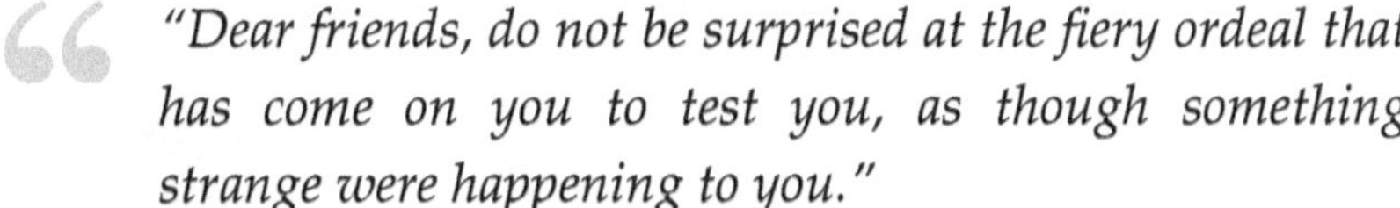

> *"Dear friends, do not be surprised at the fiery ordeal that has come on you to test you, as though something strange were happening to you."*

1 Peter 4:12 (New International Version)

There is no guarantee in this world that we will escape suffering. We won't, no matter how well we live life or love others. Hard times, suffering, and grief, major life changes, just come. God doesn't cause suffering, but knows all about it.

GET READY FOR A CHALLENGE

Both running toward and running away from a challenge are legitimate approaches. Each tactic has its own set of trials. I've encountered challenges I never thought I would face. I'm sure you have too. Life is like that. We're thrown into situations by no fault of our own, and they alter everything.

After turning that corner, we can't go back to the way things were. Any loss takes its toll; death of a loved one, a divorce you didn't ask for, or an unexpected illness that hits you from out of the blue; all bring challenges that seem like a tidal wave. We get flattened and feel as if we're being washed out to sea.

It's in these hard times, when we're sucker-punched from behind, that God can seem the most real and powerful, if we let Him. God has promised to be with us in times of new challenges or life transitions.

"Fear not, for I am with you. Do not be dismayed. I am your God. I will strengthen you; I will help you; I will uphold you with My victorious right hand."

Isaiah 41:10 (The Living Bible)

God wants us to have a certain sense of security, to "fear not." We can't see ahead, but He can.

Trusting what we can't see is an act of faith. I can't see gravity or the air we breathe. All I know is that it's there, and I couldn't live without it.

I think God wants us to dream and dream big. We're the only species capable of hope and planning for the future. We can look ahead and visualize or imagine something that hasn't happened yet, and make it happen. We can also look to the future and be paralyzed with fear, afraid of the unknown.

Do you have a strategy or a set of steps to make that dream happen? Often, the first step is the hardest and takes the most courage. A dream to unfold is a process and a long one at that. There is no magic wand to wave for our pumpkins to turn into golden coaches. And often a dream comes to us many years before it comes to life. No matter what we do, there is always preparation, and that takes time. Part of the challenge is patience.

Give yourself the time it takes for your dream or thought of a new thing to happen. See the changes in your life now as new challenges that can pour strength into places that need filling.

The challenging situations I've faced have revealed strengths in me that I had covered up with pounds of sticky, thick fear. When forced into circumstances I never thought I would face, I was made to change my clothes and try on the jacket of courage. It didn't fit very well at first, but I grew into its shape over time. I realized new dreams as I accepted the new reality of my life.

Transition into a new place in life has logical stages. Each one is like a stepping-stone that moves you through the rushing waters of change. Letting go of the thing or life as it was is the first step-ping stone. It can be a slippery place to land and a confusing, hurtful place to stay. Once our hands and hearts open to let the familiar old way fall away, we become lighter of foot to take passage into the middle place of a life transition or change.

This middle place is where discovery and patching up of our wounds can happen. Here we can look back to see the slick muddy bank from the shore we've left, but don't yet have a plan for the new way.

The middle stone in the crossing can be a large and sunny rock, a spot to rest with feet dangling in the cool waters of change. The middle is a place to re-group and formulate what the new thing in life will be. We grow and heal here, and it takes time. Don't rush off this stone.

The final stepping stone in crossing through a life transition makes passage into the new thing, the way life looks now. It took me a long time to forgo pulling out four placemats to set the dinner table after my boy died. We felt like a table with only three legs. Even small changes take time and adjustment.

No matter where you find yourself in thinking about your future, there are goals and dreams planted inside your heart. When the time is right, you'll have a glimpse of the seeds as they start to peek into your spirit.

PROMPTS 57-60

PROMPT 57

Let's write.

In thinking about the change you are going through now, do you see yourself at a particular stepping stone? Are you on the Letting Go Stone? Are you on the Middle Stepping Stone? Have you made it onto the New Thing Stone?

Do you have dreams about your future stones of change?

 *"My world was changing, and I was not ready for it."*

~ Juliet Marillier

PROMPT 58

Let's write.

Endings are unavoidable. Letting go, no matter what it consists of, leaves prints on your heart and mind that will always remain.

Can you think of a situation that ended, bringing grief or sadness, that you wouldn't trade? Describe it.

 *Don't cry because it's over, smile because it happened.*

~ Ludwig Jacobowski

PROMPT 59

Let's write.

Initially, problems might make us want to give up.

On average, which is true for you, does a problem light a fire to keep trying harder, or do you lay down a difficulty and sit on it for a while? Write about an example.

 *A problem is a chance for you to do your best.*

~ Duke Ellington

PROMPT 60

Let's write.

The safe choice in life isn't always the best. It can save a person from anticipated storms and rough waters, but it can also cause missed opportunities to be brave.

Have you stayed "in port" to avoid heading into the deep end of a circumstance or choice? What happened? Describe it.

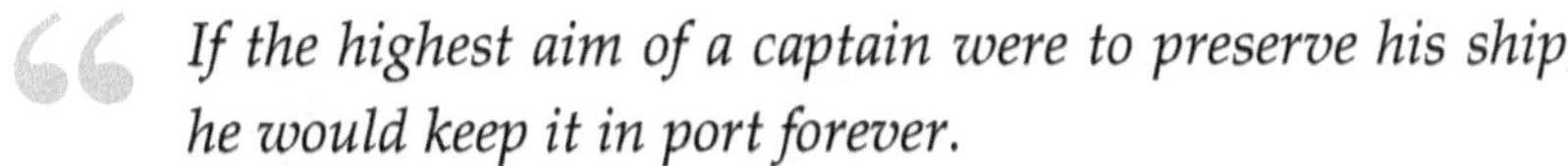

If the highest aim of a captain were to preserve his ship, he would keep it in port forever.

~ Thomas Aquinas

DAY 16: CHANGE MAKES NEW UNDERSTANDING

When life changes for better or worse, understanding the circumstances is always helpful. I knew when I got married and joined my new husband, already living in Virginia, that there would be some adjusting on my part. I was moving to a new state and a new town and taking on the new role of wife. I had my expectations of how life would be as a married lady.

It was wonderful. There is something magical about those first few months of newly married life, and then true life sets in. It was nothing serious for me; it was the reality that daily life is just that: daily. It takes understanding to live with another person: a husband, a roommate, a child, or a parent. Circles, which once stood complete on their own, now intersect with the rings of another person's life.

The problem comes when a major change that makes no sense at all hits you head-on. Those are the tough ones to understand. There are circumstances that come without insight or perspective, and we're never the same.

I DON'T GET IT

We can live without food for seven days, without water for three days, and for a lifetime with a broken heart. They say time heals all wounds, but some hurts, especially the ones we don't understand, can take residence inside us and never leave.

I've learned to live with the pieces of my heart that are missing, broken off in grief and loss. The biggest lesson: keep going without knowing the "why." I will have to wait; some answers are not found on this side of heaven.

New circumstances don't have to be understood.

Are you living with a situation that makes no sense right now? A new life will open before your eyes if you can see a way to embrace the "now," no matter what it looks like.

God, in His wisdom, equips us with the strength to accept things we can't change.

"And let us not get tired of doing what is right, for after a while we will reap a harvest of blessing if we don't get discouraged and give up."

Galatians 6:9 (The Living Bible)

Giving up and getting discouraged is the death of moving forward and growing in understanding. The problem is that it's so easy to do, and often my first line of defense. When things are hard, I don't want to have anything to do with them.

Have you felt discouraged and ready to quit dealing with your current trial? Everyone has. It's the folks who let that thinking sit for just a minute but not settle in and take root, who can press ahead, no matter what.

I want to be one of those who "reap a harvest of blessing." I don't want to get so tired and worn out from wrong thinking that I miss a bumper crop of God's good things showered on my life. Often, good things come as a surprise.

The word *blessing* is mentioned 67 times in the Bible. The word *blessed* is mentioned 302 times in the King James Version of Scripture. God wants to express His favor and happiness toward us and delights in blessing us. A harvest of blessings implies to me an overflow, full fields, and many blessings to share. We may be in a new place in our lives, a place we don't fully understand how to navigate, but God is in heaven reaping a bounty of blessings for us if we will not give up!

Wait for the harvest; there are crops just for you.

PROMPT 61-64

PROMPT 61

Let's write.

Have you felt discouraged, wanting to quit doing good, especially in a bad situation? How did you overcome and keep going?

In the past, have you experienced God pouring out His harvest of blessings on your life? If so, what did it look like?

Do you see a blessing in your current circumstance? Do you have a reaction to the statement, "New circumstances don't have to be understood?" What does that mean to you?

What kind of "new crops" are ahead for you?

It's only after you've stepped outside your comfort zone that you begin to change, grow, and transform.

~ Roy T. Bennett

PROMPT 62

Let's write.

Life is full of thorns. The barbs of disappointment, grief, or loss prick deeply. If we only look at the scar, we miss the bloom that sits atop the stem.

Have you ever gotten stuck looking at only the thorns of a circumstance and missed the joy or fragrance of the flower that caused you pain?

Write about an example.

Some people always grumble because roses have thorns; I am thankful that thorns have roses.

~ Alphonse Karr

PROMPT 63

Let's write.

A bend in the road has purpose. It could be to avoid a cliff up ahead or to take a traveler around the unseen obstacle. Bends are part of a journey; no path is ever straight without turns or twists.

Have you ever 'failed to make a turn' in your life?

What was the outcome?

 *A bend in the road is not the end of the road...Unless you fail to make the turn.*

~ Helen Keller

PROMPT 64

Let's write.

No one ever *wants* to hit bottom. Climbing high is praised and encouraged. But pride or foolish choices can loosen our fingers and cause us to crash into a heap. If you get back up, or how you bounce back up, is the difference between failure and destiny.

Do you have an example of hitting bottom and how you proceeded? Write about it.

 *I don't measure a man's success by how high he climbs but how high he bounces when he hits bottom.*

~ George S. Patton

DAY 17: CHANGE MAKES NEW PLACES

My life was not one of moving around. I was 2 years old when my family moved to the state and town where I would spend all my elementary and high school years, including two years of college. My dad was the athletic director and basketball coach at a small Christian college. My roommate was my high school best friend. Her father was the college's president. Life was full and predictable.

Then, everything changed. We, kids, were not aware of the situation that caused my dad to leave the college and move our family to a faraway southern state. We were not included in the discussion or in the circumstances that led to his position being ended. He was devastated, and so were we.

As the moving truck pulled away, for the first time, I saw my dad cry. That was a sobering moment, not forgotten. A new place to live for our family was ahead. That move proved short-lived and was used to propel the family to another town, which became their final home for over 40 years.

New places, new states, new towns, or new careers can start out as journeys filled with fear and sadness. New places can grow into just the place we are destined to be if we have the patience to wade through and let go. A new place doesn't have to be where we live: it can be who we are.

A NEW PLACE

Change shakes things up. Time has a way of moving things around; children grow up, parents age, dreams fade, and loved ones come and go. Our reality can become new. That's how we learn the lessons of transition. We move from one thing to the next in action, in situations, or even in our thoughts. Like it or not, the only option is to accept the change and adapt to the new place life gives us.

If you don't have a clear view or understanding of the bigger plan for your life right now, don't worry. That doesn't mean there isn't one.

The Apostle Paul writes,

"Now we see things imperfectly, like puzzling reflections in a mirror, but then we will see everything with perfect clarity. All that I know now is partial and incomplete, but then I will know everything completely, just as God now knows me completely."

1 Corinthians 13:12 (New Living Translation)

I know what blurred vision looks like. All I have to do is remove my glasses, and the world becomes unrecognizable and fuzzy. Life looks like that sometimes, too. It becomes unclear and distorted in the face of heartbreak, unwanted change, or fear. God stands in the middle of our incomplete lives and assures us He knows and loves us completely.

Faith takes hold to believe that, and the "puzzling reflections in the mirror" we see now will one day be well-defined and vibrant. Our knowledge and understanding of God are limited and imperfect.

The plan designed for you might be vague now, even devastating, but don't give up; a new place is promised. God keeps His promises.

When walking into uncertainty, how do you react? Do you take it on or run and hide?

I admire people who face a mountain of change and are brave right out of the box. They are energized by a challenge and embrace a new thing wholeheartedly. They are winners, leaders, and entrepreneurs. I can be those things, but I must float around on my back in the pool of indecision for a bit and take small steps. It's all about how we're wired. I'm more comfortable in the warm water of the familiar. Don't throw me in the deep end; I know how to swim, but I prefer to float.

How about you? When faced with a decision or circumstance that requires change, are you a climber, someone who hits the challenge hard? Or are you more cautious, preferring the course of change to be a slow slope with a well-defined path?

Sometimes we don't get a choice.

PROMPTS 65-69

PROMPT 65

Let's write.

Are you at a place in your life where you can see the reality of new things, new places, or new friends?

When you take on a challenge, how do you prepare? Do you want to run and hide? How does this work for you? Have you ever had a new place or circumstance that changed everything? Did your new place change your identity or how you saw your-self? How so?

If you need a kick start today, begin today's prompt by finishing this sentence:

When I'm forced to accept a hard place in my life, I…

 *"In the process of letting go you will lose many things from the past, but you will find yourself."*

~ Deepak Chopra

PROMPT 66

Let's write.

Who or what has created who you are today? How have you allowed decisions to influence a particular circumstance? Whose decisions influenced that circumstance?

If you could change those decisions, would you want to? If so, how would you imagine those different decisions playing out?

 *I am not a product of my circumstances. I am a product of my decisions.*

~ Stephen Covey

PROMPT 67

Let's write.

Have you ever thought of your life as a story to tell? It is, and it's worthy of the telling. Start here and share an account of who you are and why.

Someone needs to hear it.

 *Don't wait around for someone else to tell your story. Do it yourself by whatever means necessary.*

~ Lena Dunham

PROMPT 68

Let's write.

Pain is a teacher of many things; it chisels us with markings that produce a heart to see the hurting in others. That's a treasure.

Write about a situation where the outcome of pain also gave you courage.

Take chances, make mistakes. That's how you grow. Pain nourishes your courage. You have to fail in order to practice being brave.

~ Mary Tyler Moore

PROMPT 69

Let's write.

Do you have any years in your life where struggle can now be seen as beautiful?

Describe the situation and the beauty that was discovered.

One day, in retrospect, the years of struggle will strike you as the most beautiful.

~ Sigmund Freud

DAY 18: CHANGE MAKES NEW BEGINNINGS

Change happens, and there's no way around it. Not all change is painful or unwanted; new babies, weddings, and new jobs are a blessing! Change is necessary and represents growth and new beginnings. It's all around us. Seasons have their purpose. We would never have the boldness of fall color if cold nights didn't trigger branches to throw a last party of farewell to their leaves.

Somehow, spring buds know when to magically appear from the hard ground of winter. The warming soil gives a signal and a call to new tender life. It's always fascinated me to see those first brave buds of crocus pink and blue push their tiny heads toward the light. It's as if they couldn't stand being trapped in the dark ground one more day. It's their new beginning and our delight.

Every ending has a new beginning. Endings can be painful and blow our world apart; they leave us battle-worn and weary. How can we possibly build a new beginning from ashes that smolder, burning with fire that time doesn't seem to extinguish?

ENDINGS BRING BEGINNINGS

In my book, *Hello Nobody, Standing at the Door Alone, What to Do When Everything Changes*, I explain how afraid I was to leave my old self and life behind when unwanted life changes exploded all around me. I felt I would be somehow diminished and dismantled, as the familiar roles I signed up for were no longer mine. Circumstances erased the world I knew, and I wasn't prepared to figure out how to set out on a new course.

But I did. I started my life over, one day at a time, deciding how to shine new light into the places darkened by loss and grief. My husband was my champion, my cheerleader; he cheered me on with pom-poms of encouragement to be brave and accomplished. When cancer captured his life, I felt benched and sidelined. I became a team of one player.

Have you ever felt like a "team of one player?" Did the cheering section somehow change leagues, leaving you to go home or find a new sport? These feelings of loneliness are real, even with a large circle of loved ones surrounding your life. The emotions can be fresh or from years ago. No matter the time frame, the pain spot remains.

 *"The only way to make sense out of change is to plunge into it, move with it, and join the dance."*

~ Alan W. Watts

A new beginning in life, no matter its cause, starts out small. Imagine the size of a mustard seed. This tiny seed can grow between six and twenty feet in height! It takes the right soil and time. In Scripture, Jesus refers to this particular kernel, teaching us that even faith as small as a mustard seed can accomplish much. We often think it takes grand, large steps to move the mountains in our lives to a new place, but it doesn't.

When I was first trying to reorient my life to a new beginning, looking ahead was too overwhelming and crushing. I couldn't climb that wall! This was when I realized that God had already equipped me to walk the journey. I just needed to take small steps behind Him. He knew the pathway up and over what I couldn't see or understand. Small steps, like a tiny seed, can grow into a mighty new thing.

Have you ever thought that God could be part of your new journey? If not, I wish you would consider asking Him about it. To some, He may seem too detached and not real, something only church people know about. I challenge you; if that's what you think, take the dare to ask Him to show up in your life. If a booming voice from the heavens or a burning bush on your driveway is the only response from God that makes sense, try a softer tactic.

In times of questioning and panic over a situation, God has made Himself known by filling me with peace and comfort that makes no earthly sense. Sometimes, just when I need it most, a word of encouragement comes from the most unexpected place. God speaks more often in a whisper than a shout, and when we ask Him to be real, He will!

When you look behind, can you see the progress you've made in your journey to a new place? There's a space between what remains at our back and what lies ahead.

The view in my rear-view mirror of what has passed grows dimmer as the years pass. I was always afraid I would forget the sound of my husband's easy laugh or the feel of my little boy's arms around my neck. They have dimmed in my memory into a soft fog, blurred into a space I can no longer reach.

Time has a way of healing and also removing precious pieces of the life we took for granted. I realize it would be emotionally unhealthy to be fixated on parts of life that are no longer with me. I'm not. The scenes behind me have cloud swirling in and out of the corners of my memory, dulling the crisp points of yesterday and what was. We don't have eyes in the back of our heads for a reason. Our vision is ahead, in front of us, sharp to see where we are going, even if it's only by a single footstep.

My husband tried to teach me how to golf. "Keep your head down and keep your eye on the ball" was always his instruction. I tried, really tried, but my head just naturally came up and threw off my swing. It turned out golf was not for me, and I soon realized the cart ride was more fun than the game. Life is like that, too. Where we fix our eyes is important. What we look at turns our head, and that changes everything.

Taking on any new challenge requires determination and the will to keep trying. The payoff is a new thing cultivated; a new life takes root and grows a garden of new flowers for a different season. The past, your life or situation before, has made the soil rich and full of nutrients for this next garden of living. There will be new colors, varieties, and all kinds of opportunities to embellish and grow.

No circumstance or situation is missed or wasted by God. Every change or challenge is an opportunity for us to look outside ourselves and discover another piece of the puzzle that makes up our unique, one-of-a-kind life. If the pieces don't fit together yet, don't worry; we are all a work in progress.

No one can have as much impact on others as you can. No one has more influence or love to share in the circles that surround your life than you!

No matter how full of joy or heartache, our past has shaped us. Its chisel marks sculpt us into who we are. Those markings become the soft spots for God to mold our purpose and make us His treasure.

PROMPTS 70-73

PROMPT 70

Let's write.

Using the metaphor of fire and flames, is there an ending of something that still has hot embers (or flames) of pain for you? Describe it and all the feelings attached in as much detail as you can.

How does God show up in the middle of your messy or confusing situation? How does he join you in the flames?

New beginnings are ahead. Do you see them? What do they look like?

"Change is inevitable-except from a vending machine.

~ Robert C. Gallagher

PROMPT 71

Let's write.

Knowing that you are unique, what makes you different from everyone else in the world? Which physical differences? How is your personality unique? How has your lived experience been unlike anyone else's?

If it helps, describe yourself in third person, as if you were describing a friend or a stranger.

 *Be yourself, everyone else is taken.*

~ Oscar Wilde

PROMPT 72

Let's write.

Any change can be a tall order. It can be especially difficult to change our attitude when we don't want to.

Think of a situation where you intentionally chose to change your thinking.

What was the outcome? Did you have difficulty doing it?

 *If you don't like something, change it. If you can't change it, change your attitude.*

~ Maya Angelou

PROMPT 73

Let's write.

In thinking about the places in your life that need rebuilding, what new circumstances will you use like gravel bits to firm up courage and allow new things?

How has your support helped you stay brave during this rebuilding?

 *All that you touch*

You Change.

All that you Change

Changes you.

The only lasting truth

is Change.

God is Change.

~ Octavia E. Butler

DAY 19: CHANGE MAKES NEW WALLS

There will come a time when you are ready to pick up your life and start building it into its new shape. The nudge to do so may be shortly after a life knockout, or it may take years to feel strong enough to rebuild. But, eventually, you'll know it's a tap on your heart.

Slowly but surely, days will stack on each other like the stones in a crafted wall. The master Waller chooses just the shape and size of each rock to fit perfectly in its place. Ask anyone who has built a dry stone wall, one not using mortar or cement, to anchor the pieces, and they will share fundamental rules for lasting and safe construction. It takes time, muscle, and trial and error to build anything from the bottom up, be it a new life or a stone wall.

When rebuilding a life shattered by heartache, grief, or any change, there is a method to follow. Besides the rock's inherent durability, gravity holds the rock in place, as each one sits square on the rock below it.

Even if you don't have all the pieces lined up yet, take hold of the new life that's set before you. Set the course of the new thing you want to build and start laying a foundation.

BUILDING A NEW THING

A firm foundation is necessary for any new building project. It's a place to start building.

After the foundation is set, the next step in building a stone wall is to dig a trench to the desired depth and width. In reformatting your world, it might take some digging into places to discover "stones" that aren't needed anymore. When my family was gone, and I was living alone, I discovered that I had to rethink even the simplest task. Grocery shopping for one person is much more limited than the list for a family. I needed to adapt and rethink even such an insignificant detail.

Gravel is part of the wall-building process. It fills in uneven spots and gives solid support to start building. It must be tamped down, pounding the loose bits into the ground.

After the ground is prepared for wall making, level stones are placed as a firm base to begin the often slow process of building. Each stone at this stage must be leveled and placed side to side snugly. As we rebuild our new wall of life, we also need the stability of others alongside us. Family, friends, and community give us a snug place to build and move forward. Loose stones at this stage are unsettling and can cause uneven footing as we build our new life.

For stones to stay firmly in place without the glue of cement, the waller must be skilled at cutting rocks to achieve a perfect fit and placement. It isn't known which stone will fit where until the moment it's needed. Life is like that, too. If we're open to allowing change into unfamiliar places, there is no telling what a perfect fit it will become. It's easy to keep looking for the familiar, the thing we know, even if it doesn't fit in the new wall.

Drainage and backfill come next in stone wall building. A buried PVC pipe carries water away from the wall, minimizing damage. Backfilling with dirt helps stabilize the structure. When life changes beneath us, the new life we build becomes more permanent and secure if we include the strengths and supports of determination and faith as our backfill. These supports keep us stable even when life feels unsure and full of missing pieces.

PROMPTS 74-77

PROMPT 74

Let's write.

Creating something new often takes a plan and a purpose. How would you describe your process of remaking your new world? If you're building a new foundation, what is this new one made of? How is it different from your old foundation?

List the benefits of behind-the-scenes support in your journey to a new place in your life.

Broken hearts hurt but they make you strong.

~ Unknown

PROMPT 75

Let's write.

Hope is an expectation that something will change. It's full of promise. Hopelessness carries a heavy burden of despair and distress. If something is 'right,' it lightens the strain and makes the decision or the circumstance easier to grasp.

Have you given up on something that seemed 'hopeless' despite it being 'right'?

Today, write about that.

Nothing is hopeless that is right.

~ Susan B. Anthony

PROMPT 76

Let's write.

We are a mix of many parts, many loved ones, many experiences, many preferences, and so much more. What are those parts? Who contributed to them?

When the "ordinary" you is given a chance to appear, have any pieces of those many parts surprised you? What are those parts? Write about it.

We are all ordinary. We are all boring. We are all spectacular. We are all shy. We are all bold. We are all heroes. We are all helpless. It just depends on the day.

~ Brad Meltzer

PROMPT 77

Let's write.

The future doesn't belong to us, but we can see it. Have you been putting anything off, waiting for a later day? Is today the day to start a new thing?

Write about that.

> *Someday is not a day of the week.*
>
> ~ Janet Dailey

DAY 20: CHANGE MAKES NEW RELATIONSHIPS

Relationships with other people give purpose, flavor, and most of all structure to our lives. We are created to have connections with others. Love is a human need like food, water, and air. Babies, left alone, not given human touch or nurturing, grow up emotionally stunted or die. There is a condition called "failure to thrive" in infants that is directly linked to being neglected, not touched, and missing affectionate parental care.

We need each other. We need love and to be loved. A relationship is the state of being connected. When our familiar connections break or dissolve due to a life change or grief, a hole is torn open, leaving us wounded. Part of the healing process is to rebuild. Some losses can be recreated. A new job might turn out to be more satisfying than the last. The end of a difficult marriage could lead to a happy, satisfying union.

Some losses can never be replaced and have the added challenge of learning to live with the void. I'll never forget someone told me just after my son died, "Don't worry, you are young, you can have more children." I was so taken aback by her senseless comment that I had no reaction except to think about how impossible it is to replace one person with another. People are not interchangeable.

As relationships come and go in life, there are those of family and dear friends that make up the framework of our world. These are the people we live with, depend on, and cherish. They pour into our lives like Plaster of Paris into a mold. They give us strength and help shape who we become.

New relationships can come from anywhere if we're open and notice them. Some of my dearest friends were people I met by chance and with whom I instantly connected. We're still good friends years later. We can never have too many people in our lives who love us. And the more people we love back, the deeper our own well of love becomes. Pouring love out to others allows love to come in and refill our tank.

PROMPTS 78-81

PROMPT 78

Let's write.

If you could design a new relationship with someone, what would it look like? What would this person be: male or female, younger than you or older, or the same age? What interests, hobbies, or jobs would they have? Think about meeting this new person. How did it happen? What attracted you to them? What is it you think you like about them? Imagine as much detail as possible.

Now, thinking of this imaginary person, write a piece about what this person thinks of YOU. Write it from their perspective as if they were writing about you. What would they say about you? What would they be attracted to about you? How did they meet you?

Have fun with this and see what your imaginary friend thinks of you!

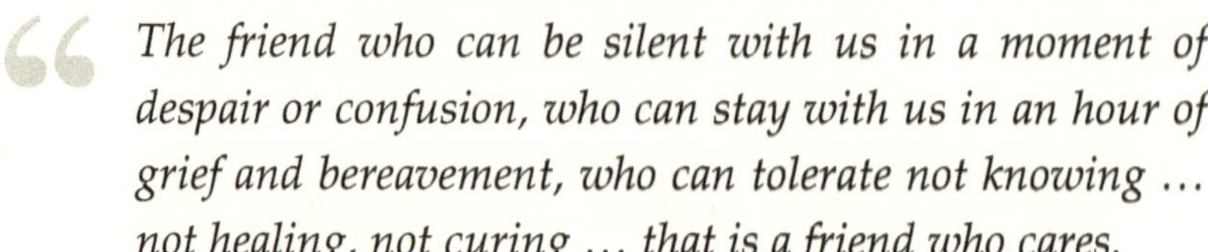

The friend who can be silent with us in a moment of despair or confusion, who can stay with us in an hour of grief and bereavement, who can tolerate not knowing … not healing, not curing … that is a friend who cares.

~ Henri Nouwen

PROMPT 79

Let's write.

Write about an accomplishment that has brought you the changes of acknowledgement from others or another kind of reward.

How does your opinion of that accomplishment vary from others? If you could attempt this again, how might you do it differently?

The reward of a thing well done is having done it.

~ Ralph Waldo Emerson

PROMPT 80

Let's write.

What do you think the above quote is implying? Do you see yourself as the 'candle' or the 'mirror' in terms of shedding light? Explain your choice.

 *There are two way of spreading light; to be the candle, or the mirror that reflects it.*

~ Edith Wharton

PROMPT 81

Let's write.

A time might come when it's easy to think age has stepped in front of you to stop you from dreaming or making new goals.

Imagine yourself 15 years older than you are now.

Where do you picture yourself? What are you doing? Do you have a new passion? Describe.

 *You are never too old to set another goal or dream a new dream.*

~ C.S. Lewis

DAY 21: CHANGE
MAKES NEW IDENTITY

As months span into years, your new life will grow and take root. These shoots reach into the soil of today and mature from nutrients buried in the shade of the past. Life will expand into places bursting with possibility. Our past is never wasted, no matter how hard it is.

Such an opportunity is built one stone at a time. The Master Builder has a plan and a purpose for each of us, even if our lives in the past have become a pile of rubble. God has a way of rebuilding the wall and repurposing each broken section. Let Him have the chisel and the backhoe. He has the tools to remake you into the person you were meant to be.

On a hiking trail, there is usually a marked start and a finish. A map will indicate the trailhead and the route back. God knows your personal trailhead. He was at your start and hiked next to you, opening doors and clearing the path of downed trees and boulders. He sees the potential and the purpose inside each of us.

My life, as possibly yours, isn't what I thought it would be. I've had to take hard turns and exit ramps I didn't want to take. But the end of the story isn't written yet. All I can say for sure now is that I have a deeper well of love and need for God to be part of my life. It has come from the desperate times when everything crashed to the floor. I had to pick myself up and stand to face one heartbreak after another.

My son died in his sleep at age nine; my husband lost his battle with cancer; I had my own fight with breast cancer; my daughter moved far out of state for her own life, and my dear parents are waiting for me in heaven. As my career ended, I found myself writing the book *Hello Nobody, Standing at the Door Alone, What to do When Everything Changes.*

At each of these life-altering circumstances, I had to take on new roles as my identity changed and developed. Just as a snake must leave its old skin to live, we often must leave what is known and familiar and let the new skin of who we are grow into place.

PROMPT 82

Let's write.

Sit in a comfortable spot, alone if that's possible. You have accomplished 21 days of taking stock of your life, spreading it out on paper. It might be exactly what you thought it would look like, or there might have been some surprises along the way. In either case, good job at getting to this page!

Journal for as long as you need to sum up what you have learned about yourself or your life in these past 21 days. No one needs to read your work unless you choose to share it.

In the last 21 days, I have learned…

You are so brave and quiet, I forgot you were suffering.

~ Ernest Hemingway

PROMPT 83

Let's write.

Which virtue(s) do you value the most? The least? Why or why not?

Do you have an example of those virtues standing tall within your life?

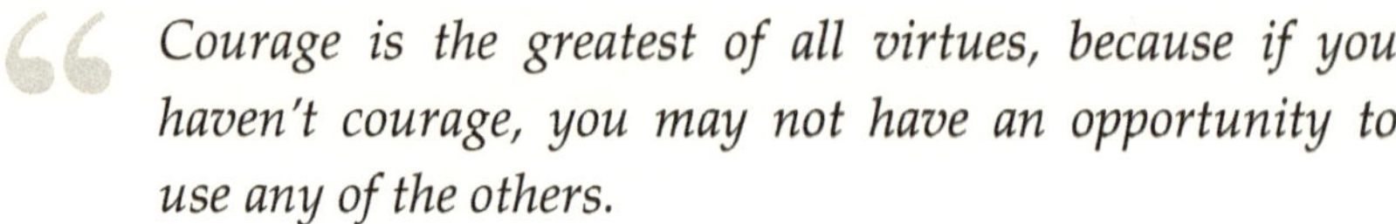

Courage is the greatest of all virtues, because if you haven't courage, you may not have an opportunity to use any of the others.

~ Samuel Johnson

PROMPT 84

Let's write.

Write about an incident from your life where you found yourself rising from a failure.

Did you discover the glory of that rising?

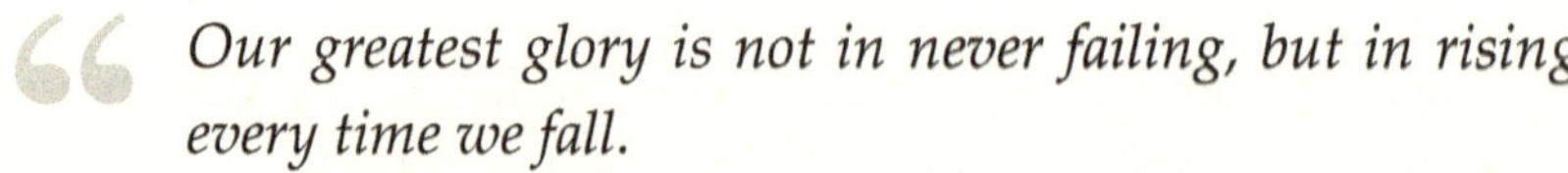

Our greatest glory is not in never failing, but in rising every time we fall.

~ Confucius

PROMPT 85

Let's write.

What is the metaphorical weather of change like in your life today? Is the sun shining? Is the wind howling?

Describe the landscape. If needed, use your five senses to spark greater detail.

The time to repair the roof is when the sun is shining.

~ John F. Kennedy

CLOSING LETTER

 *A ship in the port is safe, but not what ships are built for.*

~William G.T. Shedd

Congratulations! Regardless of how long it took you to complete this journal, you are accomplished. I hope the questions and writing prompts helped smooth out a few rough patches in your seasons of change. Perhaps it provided a spot to get some clarity about your journey?

Hopefully, as you worked through the *Write Your Way Through Change*, you discovered the value of writing. Journaling is a powerful tool, no matter how often you write. I have friends who write only through a crisis, and others who must journal every day or burst.

Grief is a shirt we wear for a long time. It starts out ill-fitting and full of holes. As time goes on, we grow into it and learn to live out the lessons born of hard times. Eventually, the garment of grief can be traded in for acceptance and peace about what such a life upheaval produced. The pain it creates is real, but can soften into pools of new understanding and hopefully, a whole new you.

If you haven't yet, you're invited to read my story through this change. My book, *Hello Nobody: Standing at the Door Alone, What to Do When Everything Changes*, is available on my website and Amazon. (https://jhaney.com) I know what it's like to lose everything you held dear, only to feel like you're facing life on your own.

Having gone through my journey with grief and transition, my lasting promise to you is that God is real. He has walked beside you in silent and majestic ways during your travels in this season of change. You may not even have been aware of the arm around you and of His call to know Him better. Don't waste the pain. It can be used for the biggest call on your heart, the one with eternal benefit.

The highway through grief or a major life transition is never easy. The thoroughfare is full of twists and turns, steep hills, and scary valleys. We slip on icy patches of uncertainty and get blinded by the fog of our broken hearts. Just know, eventually the dust settles and reveals the new place change has built.

The change may be smaller than we expected, or it may be brighter, with a brilliance never imagined. There's no way of knowing for sure what passageway our brokenness will discover.

I encourage you to continue expanding the horizons of your writing and to explore the benefits writing can bring to your life. The paybacks are plenty: sanity, clarity of mind, creative flow, emotional release, and even an answer.

Most importantly, a deeper walk and relationship with God, who understands everything, especially our hardest times, can be the result. They become His treasure because in mending our broken places, we can be made new by His love.

Feel free to contact me at my website (https://www.jhaney.com), but most of all, keep writing your way through your change. Remember, your past is never wasted.

*L*et's keep writing.

~ Janet

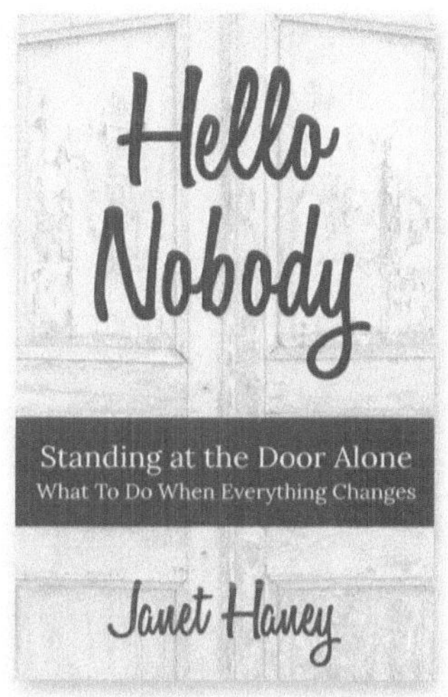

Hello Nobody: Standing at the Door Alone, What to Do When Everything Changes

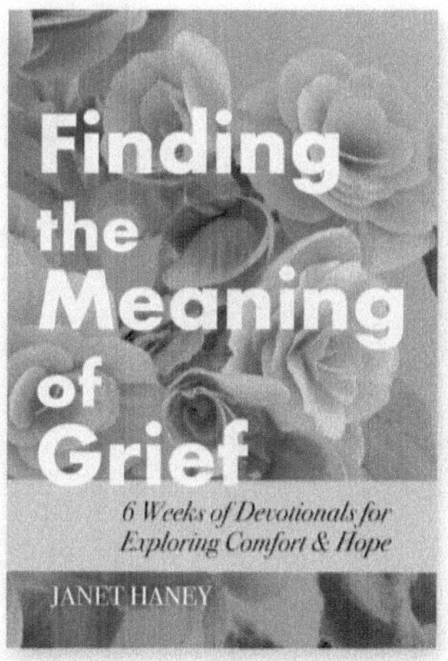

Finding the Meaning of Grief: 6 Weeks of Devotionals for Exploring Comfort & Hope

Janet Haney's grief is not tied with a neat and tidy bow. And yet it brings a healing balm of camaraderie to the heartache of every reader. Reading her story will give readers someone to stand alongside who has discovered that courage comes while walking the trail set before us.

Join her, then tell your own story.

JANET HANEY'S BOOKS ARE AVAILABLE AT:

https://jhaney.com